THRUST 2
A MEMORY

RICHARD NOBLE, OBE

AMBERLEY

First published 2022

Amberley Publishing
The Hill, Stroud
Gloucestershire, GL5 4EP

www.amberley-books.com

Copyright © Richard Noble, OBE, 2022

The right of Richard Noble, OBE to be identified
as the Author of this work has been asserted in
accordance with the Copyrights, Designs and
Patents Act 1988.

ISBN 978 1 3981 1110 3 (print)
ISBN 978 1 3981 1111 0 (ebook)

British Library Cataloguing in Publication Data.
A catalogue record for this book is available from
the British Library.

Typesetting by SJmagic DESIGN SERVICES, India.
Printed in the UK.

Contents

Introduction

In the last century Britain achieved a large number of the world land speed records, of which the country can be very proud. These records advanced knowledge and technology, and were financed by wealthy backers at a time when national resources were very unevenly shared.

The previous British land speed record was 403 mph in 1964. The innovative Americans then introduced the jet and rocket-powered challengers, and by 1970 had raised the record by over 50 per cent.

This is the story of a small group whose only start-up resource was £175 from the sale of the first Thrust car (which was dangerous) to a scrapyard. The project had to be marketed to nearly 300 sponsors for its very limited resources and finance – a difficult and demanding process, but one that insured the project was safe, competitive and the engineering achievable and audited.

As a result of this process and the brilliance of designer John Ackroyd, – the Thrust 2 car was designed and built to very high standards and achieved a world record of 633 mph. So thorough was the car's design and build that it could be driven to a lateral accuracy of 40 mm at record speeds. On test it could be driven almost every day to

Project Thrust logo.

over 600 mph and, unlike most land speed record cars, it achieved its design speed of 650 mph.

It was a huge privilege to work in the Thrust team all those years ago. We learned a lot together, and today the survivors always try to meet up every year.

The whole process from the Thrust 1 to Thrust 2 world record took nine very intense years. The Thrust 2 record was to stand for fourteen years until we took it with the ThrustSSC supersonic car – and that world record has never been beaten.

Writing this book has been difficult, not because of the fine research sources but because it includes so many personal memories without evidence. This was because the workload was so intense that there was no time for a diary or personal photos. The book draws material from private books and sources: John Ackroyd, *Just for the Record* (1984); David Tremayne, *The Fastest Man on Earth* (1986); Mike Barrett, *Thrust 2: A Record with a Different Spin* (2013); Gordon Flux, *Building Thrust 2 and Setting the Land Speed Record at 623mph in 1983* (1993); Lucas Girling, and *Project Thrust Reports 1982 and 1983* by Glynne Bowsher.

The book is dedicated to memories of the Thrust 2 team no longer with us, and to surviving Thrust 2 team members. The dedication also goes to my family who stood by me throughout the intensely difficult, strenuous and very demanding times and joined in to help us through to the world record.

This book gives us all an important opportunity. An opportunity to review the Thrust 2 project with the perspectives we have had from the later projects, and I have included Chapter 10 to try and achieve this.

Richard Noble

Chapter 1
650 mph on the Speedo

It's late afternoon in the Black Rock Desert, Nevada, and we have made the first run. It wasn't what we had hoped for – just 624.241 mph in the measured mile and 626.240 mph in the kilo. We knew this was to be the key day; we had worked on the Thrust 2 programme for six years and now it had come down to this. Winter was coming to Nevada, and with it rain and snow. We were using the maximum power possible from Thrust 2's Rolls-Royce Avon 302 engine, liberated from the Lightning F6 fighter, and we were using the longest possible run in distance – and all at full 35,000 thrust horsepower available from just a few feet after letting the brakes off. We were at the absolute limit of what was possible. Gary Gabelich's world record of 1970 was 622.407 mph for the mile and 630.389 for the kilometre, and those were the average of the times of the two mandatory passes over the distances sanctioned and confirmed by the Fédération Internationale de l'Automobile. To claim the record we would have to achieve a speed a clear 1 per cent faster. It didn't look good; in fact, it looked like six very hard years of wasted lives. The team were quiet, and we were getting ready for the mandatory return run. There was calm, but high, tension – this was it!

Last day on the Black Rock Desert.

Land speed record first run, Black Rock, 4 October 1983.

But we hadn't counted on nature – the local temperature suddenly climbed 3 degrees, which raised the speed of sound and the point at which the huge transonic aero wave drag kicked in. Thrust 2 was always a transonic car, limited by the Mach number at which it would encounter the massive aero drag rise. Of course, the team all knew that the south end of the course was much harder than the crumbly northern section, which had compromised the first run. What wasn't apparent was that designer John Ackroyd and team manager Ken Norris had extended the southern run-up distance to 6⅛ miles. We would be accelerating flat out for 7⅛ miles, but would our fuel tanks carry enough for 59 seconds of max afterburner? With these extended run-ups our fuel system was now limited by capacity. This level of engine power requires serious fuel flow, and the engine drinks jet A fuel at over a gallon a second. Concerned about excessive downforce at the front of the car, Ackroyd had changed the car incidence by +0.17 degrees, so now it was ever so slightly running nose up. We could only guess the effect this would have; it would certainly reduce the rolling resistance from the front wheels, but the aero forces at these speeds are huge and there was no time for additional wind tunnel testing to predict the effect of Johns changes – the car could easily fly very fast and very high if we had it wrong.

The turnaround team had the car refuelled and the brake parachute system rearmed. The trusty Palouste gas turbine starter from HMS *Ark Royal* connected via its long, flexy air hose. We had to wait while Walt, in his trusty Cessna aircraft, tracked up and down the course to check for any stray visitors. Walt confirmed it was all clear and we were within the 60-minute record turnaround time allowance. It was time to go, and the canopy was shut.

Push the starter button and the Palouste external gas turbine starter accelerates to a howl. The air hose jumps with the air pressure and the huge Avon engine rumbles into life. Watch it to 10 per cent of the maximum rpm and then push down with the right foot to pass the first accelerator detent and open the high-pressure fuel cock. Fuel flows into the combustion chambers and the ignition system lights up. The huge engine now takes on a new life, a protesting rumble, and then with smooth acceleration to 40 per cent its idling speed. Precious fuel is flowing now and the turnround team race to disconnect the Palouste and replace the access panel. At 40 per cent the car is going nowhere, but it makes sense to position the left foot on the brake pedal and hold hard.

Checks completed and with radio clearance confirmed, it's time to go. Take the engine up to 92 per cent and hold on the brakes for one last check. Any higher engine rpm and the car will go with brakes and wheels locked. With checks completed its brakes off and slam the accelerator through the second detent to light the afterburner. The engine roars up to 104 per cent and there is a very slight pause while the exhaust nozzle opens right out, then the Avon 302 afterburner lights with a massive shove in the back and we are off.

The acceleration, at over 2G, is relentless. The Avon doesn't run out of revs like a piston engine and now we are in the difficult sub-300 mph speed range. Thrust 2 runs on 30-inch diameter, all-aluminium wheels – they don't grip the Nevada playa surface like a tyre on tarmac. And because the speed is relatively low Ackroyd's famous twin tailfins are having difficulty keeping the car straight. We are running down a 50-foot-wide, 13-mile track and if the car migrates into another parallel track we will have lost position and will have to scrap the precious run, and one before it. It's just the normal difficult, unpredictable time with plenty of steering action to keep us in the lane just hoping that we can get through to the 350-mph zone when the fins begin to do their stuff and the car settles down.

We are into the 350-mph zone now and the engine seems to come on song like an enormous organ pipe, and we are trailing 30 feet of spectacular flame behind. Thrust 2 runs very true with a variance of 1.5 inches from the course line. But today we have a new problem, as we work our way through the 400s my helmet begins to move and to ratchet my Panotex fireproof balaclava down my face – the eye holes move downwards and I have to raise my chin to get clear vision ahead.

500 mph seems slow, but there are no trees with which to reference the speed, though the Sierra Nevada mountains change shape and perspective very quickly. There is a small wave of white condensation attaching itself to the upper lip of the intake – It always happens around 550 mph – and it appears to extend backwards towards the fins, but I can only move my eyes for a millisecond to check. It is caused by the supersonic shockwave, which attaches to the upper intake. The airflow is going supersonic and the white mist I can just see is the condensation in the low-pressure zone behind the shock. It also means that the airflow is being locally accelerated supersonic over my cockpit roof and below the car – but the car itself is a long way away from being supersonic. The next shocks are due at 615 mph when they establish over the top of the front wheel arch bodywork.

Looking ahead we are coming up to the start of the measured mile and the first timing lights. Dave Petrali and Don McGregor, the USAC timekeepers, are there anxiously checking the computers. We are right on the ragged edge and no one can afford to fail right now. The car has never been so fast. At this speed everything appears to be happening in slow motion; there is plenty of time and I can see every detail on the track as it comes up and goes under the car. All I can do here is to steer straight and get us through to the end of the measured mile and into the real danger zone.

We need to nurse the engine, which is running hotter and faster than in a Lightning fighter. We come out of the measured mile at a speed that the instruments suggest is 650 mph and we have to slow very cautiously – the aero drag builds up at the front of the car and there is danger of going sideways. I come back on the throttle to the second detent and this cancels the afterburner. Now we really are in real danger: the engine is slowing so the engine down force on the front wheels is reducing just at a time when the car incidence has been raised to reduce the load on the front and we don't know how it is going to behave. Over the seemingly endless period of counting up to 3 seconds, I have to be prepared for sudden diverge – if you can possibly prepare for something that might happen in microseconds. Without the afterburner the car is slowing and the drag is building up at the front and it could skew us out of line. We are on tiptoe and its seriously dangerous. After the 3-second count I pull the throttle back past the second detent, which cuts the fuel to the engine. There is more danger here: the engine is slowing and no longer sucking in the vast qualities of air, and there is now no power to offset the aero drag. This could cause the car to diverge (turn away from the centre line) and then we get a diagonal airflow across the top of the car, which causes lift and the car flies big time – high and very fast.

So it's crucial to fire the brake parachute immediately after you cut the fuel. The 7-foot, 6-inch-diameter supersonic nuclear bomb Irvin chute comes out on its 200-foot nylon line with an almighty crash and the car loses speed at over 5.5 g – that's over 125 mph/s – and I am braced for the Somatogravic illusion. This is a frightening experience; the excessive deceleration affects your vestibular system and conflicts the brain. The impression is that Thrust 2 is hurtling vertically down a mineshaft to the centre of the world. It is frightening because you are out of control, but the car is safe because it is hanging on the brake parachute line and staying within the desert lane. The Somatogravic has gone in an instant because we are down to 400 mph in a second or so, and that seems incredibly boring after all the transonic excitement.

At 400 mph the little 7-foot chute isn't doing too much, but gradually we are down to 300 mph. There is a great urge to apply the wheel brakes and bring everything to a stop, but if I do that I'll cook Glynne Bowsher's brakes again, and that would mean an unpopular rebuild. 200 mph now and I can bring in the wheel brakes and bring the car to a stop with a final jerk on the desert. I quickly run through the shutdown checklist and in a few minutes of sudden calm our fire crew, Mike Hearn and John Griffiths, are alongside in the Firechase Jaguar.

'That was a fast one!' said Mike. And at that moment Don McGregor from the timing stand was on the radio to everyone: 'Speed for the mile 642.971 mph. That's a new record – congratulations!'

The next day the weather broke and winter descended on Nevada – we only ever had the one chance! But we had the world record. It had only taken nine years.

650-mph return record run, 4 October 1983.

Timekeeper discussion with Don McGregor, 1983. (USAC)

fédération internationale du sport automobile

RECORD CERTIFICATE

GROUP: SPECIAL VEHICLES   **CATEGORY:** C   **CLASS:** JET

NAME: RICHARD NOBLE

VEHICULE: THRUST 2

PLACE AND DATE: BLACK ROCK DESERT : 4-10- 1983

DISTANCE: 1 MILE   **TIME:** 5.683 secs

AVERAGE SPEED: 633.468 m.p.h. WORLD RECORD

CERTIFICATE ISSUED ON:

18 November 1983

THE PRESIDENT OF THE FISA

FISA record certificate.

Chapter 2
World Record? No Previous Experience Necessary

Why is there so much excitement about the world land speed record? It's a challenge in which Britain has been a world leader. By the time we started the Thrust 2 programme there had been sixty-five successful international challenges and the record, started by the French in 1898, had now reached 622.047 mph and was held by the American Blue Flame team and driver Gary Gabelich. The British had not taken part since Donald Campbell's controversial 403 mph in 1964 and there was a vast, almost impossible, experience and technology gap to bridge. Our sole asset was £175 funding from the scrapyard who had bought the crashed remains of Thrust 1.

1974, where it all started. Thrust 1 Derwent 8 jet engine and chassis frame.

So while the earlier British records were taken with wheel-driven cars, which accelerate slowly and are fearfully expensive, the Fédération Internationale de l'Automobile had introduced Class C, which no longer required wheel drive. But the important lack of detailed ruling defined the world land speed record as the real thing – unlimited racing. Design, build and run your car, innovate, take both the risk and the consequences, do something that had never been done before.

The Thrust programme had started with Thrust 1, a dangerous home-built car that was no more than a GKN light truck chassis, minimal bodywork, no suspension and a Rolls-Royce Derwent 8 Gloster Meteor engine together with its jet pipe. It was crude, dangerous and just about everything about it was uncertain. We were fortunate enough to do outline wind tunnel work at British Aerospace to check that it wouldn't fly. We had run it at a Brands Hatch meeting, made a BBC TV item with runs at RAF St Athan, where Jim Matthews, the last surviving Derwent engine specialist, kindly helped with the engine installation and first runs. The ambition was the British land

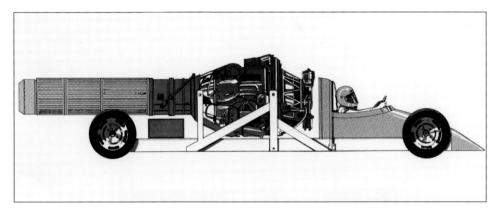

Above: Thrust 1 in Filton Wind Tunnel, 1976.

Right: Thrust 1 model in the British Aerospace Filton wind tunnel.

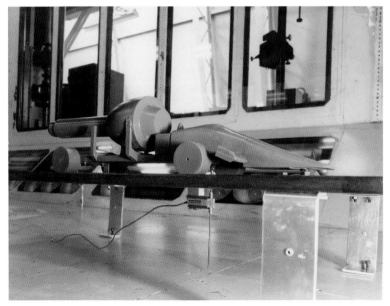

Thrust 1 engine tests, RAF St Athan.

speed record, and the chosen venue was the as yet unopened M11 motorway, but the civil servants were cautious and it never happened. Thrust 1 last ran at RAF Fairford in March 1977 – we did one good run but the return run ended in a triple airborne gyro roll. Its next destination was the scrapyard. The scrappie was keen to run up the engine, but changed his mind when we explained that the engine was shock loaded and the ignition system could kill him.

So now we were headed for Thrust 2 and the world record, which required two passes over the measured mile within 60 minutes and an average speed of at least 629 mph. We would have to extend the £175 opening cash balance to at least £1 million. Big changes were needed. We needed an outline design and a highly skilled engineer. Art Arfons of Akron Ohio had held the record three times and was the rare combination of designer builder and driver. In order to get his ferocious J-79-powered Green Monster challenger into his transportation bus he designed the car as a short challenger with himself driving from alongside the huge jet engine. This turned out to be a brilliant move. He had no engine intake problems; he could line up the car on the desert using his eyeline along the engine nacelle; and when it came to his huge and terrible 600-mph accident in 1966 he was able to survive the world's fastest car crash. His wife wasn't thrilled because he failed to call her from hospital. This gave us no more than a rough sketch for Thrust 2: a big British Avon from a Lightning supersonic fighter, single shark fin tail, a large forward wing and six wheels, with four at the front like a Tyrell P34 F1 race car. It was never going to work, but the CG and driver were in the right places, the engine was the right choice, and the layout was a winner. It just needed a highly experienced engineer to sort it out. And it needed luck and money.

Thrust 1 ready to go, RAF Fairford, 1977.

The end of Thrust 1, RAF Fairford, 1977. Next stop: the scrapyard.

Back in 1977, the year we had lost Thrust 1, I was invited to meet the RAF's head of public relations, Air Commodore Paddy Hine. The Royal Air Force was having a rough time with public relations – no one appeared interested in promoting the frightening consequences of nuclear war. Public relations were essential to the force's morale and it was a really difficult time for everyone.

'How can we help you?' asked Paddy. I unrolled the drawing. 'We need a Lightning fighter.' It was a simple ask. The Lightning Mach 2 supersonic fighter was coming to the end of its operational life and they had to be swept up somewhere, if only to the scrappies.

One thing led to another and by cashing in everything I had I was able to buy a Rolls-Royce Avon 2010. The engine was delivered to my home in Twickenham and was stored in the garage –symbolic of our determination to see this through to record success. There was now absolutely no money, but we had the Avon. We just needed a brilliant engineer to make all this work.

Of course there was no money for an advert, so we put out a press release: 'Wanted 650mph Car Designer.' By sheer good fortune it made the *Daily Telegraph* and *Cars and Car Conversions (Triple C)* – the monthly must read for all ambitious home car designers and engineers. *The Telegraph* column produced a crop of fantastically expensive engineers with impressive CVs, and an accountant who could not believe the project could be done on £175 starting. But *Triple C* produced John Ackroyd.

All this was developing with friendly consulting from Ken Norris, designer of the brilliant K7 Bluebird boat and the CN7 wheel-driven land speed record car of 1964.

Donald Campbell's chief mechanic, Leo Villa, had also been incredibly helpful. Leo and I spent a memorable evening in his Reigate home and all the Campbell stories poured out – there were real gems of instruction, which were to stand us all in good stead in the years to come. 'Always go for more power than you think you need,' Leo advised.

Leo was still going strong at 3 a.m. the next morning, but my head was buzzing and I couldn't absorb any more, so, with apologies, I bailed out and went home. Simple advice from these giants of record-breaking turned out to be incredibly important and enabled us to make what turned out to be correct decisions time and time again.

John Ackroyd was angry: he had applied for the job and heard nothing. It wasn't surprising because my day job required extensive overseas travel and was incredibly demanding. I made a promise to invite Ken Norris to interview him. We were two days late getting through to Ken to initiate the interview: 'He's already here,' said a surprised Ken.

John and I needed to get started, but we needed money and there wasn't much left of the £175. David Benson, motoring editor of the *Daily Express* and close friend of Donald Campbell, really understood record-breaking and offered us 1,000 square feet of Earl's Court exhibition space for their new national car show, MotorFair 1977. We had to go for it big time – it was a unique opportunity. But John had to go contracting

John Ackroyd, Ken Norris and Richard Noble with CN-7 and Thrust 2 models, 1981.

MotorFair, Earl's Court, 1977.

with Porsche, where there was a massive advantage in the Porsche extensive technical library.

The huge Motorfair stand was on the first floor of the Earl's Court exhibition, and we really had to make our presence felt. The stand was designed by George Myers and my employers, GKN Mills, built the stand structure. We had the 25-foot Avon engine from the upper installation of a Lightning down one side of the stand. We achieved a confirmation of television coverage and sold advertising panels down each side. The stand would feature a wide screen and Cygnet Guild's astonishing land speed record film, *The Fastest Man on Earth*, complete with ultra-high-powered amplification. My

The first 1,000 members of the public join up. Motorfair, 1997.

brother-in-law Alan Bruford ran the stand for ten desperate days. By the end of the show he had seen the film over 100 times. We knew we had it right when the Guards Regimental band complained from downstairs that the sound was so loud they were having difficulty playing. It clearly wasn't loud enough, so we turned it up! Every 10 minutes or so we would stop the film and call for the public to join the Supporters Club. By the end of MotorFair we had real media awareness, 36,000 stand visitors, 1,000 paid-up members and a real task force.

But that wasn't the high spot. Earlier that summer John Newble, the publicity director of TI Reynolds, was showing interest. John Ackroyd had already decided to design the car with the three-dimension space frame in Reynolds' 531 Manganese Molybdenum steel tube – the famous steel tube of choice for performance bicycle design and for the engine space frame for the E-Type Jaguar. There was another enormous advantage: TI Reynolds employed Ken Sprayson, the most famous frame fabricator, who could be seen at every Isle of Man TT repairing overstressed racer's frames.

John Newble and his team were to due join the stand at some stage on the MotorFair Press day. He was late and we fretted that he had probably found better entertainment on the ground floor. He eventually arrived, together with his PR agency team, and they looked around in amazement. The stand was processing over 3,500 visitors a day, crammed into the small cinema space, and this came with a steady flow of noise complaints from both floors of the Earl's Court show. But our neighbouring stand

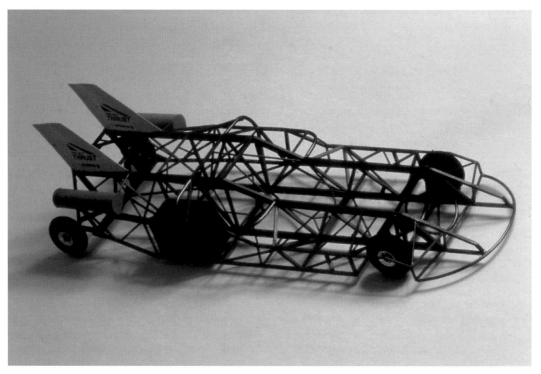

Ackroyd's space frame model, 1979.

operators on the second floor soon woke up to the benefit: we were attracting the public up from the ground floor in large numbers.

Newble had seen – and heard – enough. He was impressed and was about to leave – we were about to lose him. We quickly invited him and his team to lunch at one of the expensive peripheral Earl's Court restaurants, and Ken Norris spent ages carefully briefing them on the realities of record-breaking. 'OK,' said Newble, 'TI Reynolds will build your space frame.'

The time came to pay the restaurant bill – £65! That was precisely our current balance. We were deeply excited; not only were we insolvent, but the whole deal had paid off and now we could build the car. We had the jet engine and now we would get the huge space frame built by the one and only Ken Sprayson.

Over in Stuttgart, John was hard at work on the Porsche Ambulance by day and Thrust 2 by night, and access to the Porsche library was really paying off.

The first financial sponsor in was Loctite UK, a company we would get to know really well over the years. The Loctite funds were key in liberating John from Porsche. Seeing that we had the engine, the space frame and some of John's time, Loctite took the gamble and signed for the first year.

John had made it plain that he wanted to build Thrust 2 on the Isle of Wight. At first it seemed a strange choice, but gradually it dawned on us that this was a smart move. The Isle of Wight had a tremendous history of boat and aircraft manufacture, in particular Saunders-Roe, which had built the Princess flying boat and the SR.53 mixed

Ken Sprayson builds the Thrust 2 space frame, TI Reynolds, 1977.

Loctite cutaway poster, 1982.

powerplant fighter on which John had worked. The Isle of Wight has a favourable climate and is a really nice place to set up home. This meant that many of John's apprentice friends, like Tony Peters and Mike Horne, had set up small industries, and so there was an amazing and very capable industrial infrastructure already in place.

We rented the kitchen of a derelict house at Ranalagh works in Fishourne for £5 per week in May 1978, and John moved in with the largest drawing board any of us had ever seen. It was a very tough start as we had minimal funds, but John was astonishingly productive and the drawings kept coming, even though we couldn't

The start of Thrust 2: John at his Ranalagh design office, 1978.

afford a telephone and John had to cycle 5 miles to Bembridge to get his drawings copied at the Britten-Norman aircraft company.

So, the project development programme became clear: I had to make the money in London and the mainland and John would spend it on the island. There was huge mutual trust, and we set up an ambitious relationship where John had to build the car as fast as he could and I had to match him with the money. It was the only way to work quickly and, of course, this would lead to a string of cash and production crises, but our rules were that the car progress had to advance as quickly as we could and our team had to be paid.

Just after John moved into Ranalagh, I was down on the island and John passed me a teacup-sized, freshly cadmium-plated metal component with a gauze centre. 'What's that?' I asked. 'The first piece of the car – a fuel tank breather.' Holding it in my hand, it was difficult to believe that somehow we would finance and build a 27-foot monster car with 35,000 horsepower and capable of cruising faster than a Boeing 747.

In the meantime, we had signed the contract with TI Reynolds and Ken Sprayson was underway with what has to be one of the largest car space frames ever. Thrust 2 would be 27 feet long and 8 feet 4 inches wide, and its afterburner flame would be another 30 feet. This violent machine seemed out of place in the peaceful surroundings of the leafy Isle of Wight.

It was about this time that John had a brilliant idea that would have enormous consequences. He wanted to make my driver's seat. It seemed out of place and out of the build sequence at the time, but we went ahead. And thank God we did.

Chapter 3
Where's the Money?

It's still 1978 and John is sweating it out in the derelict house kitchen in front of his massive drawing board. The whole project was an enormous act of personal faith between us. John was designing in the office kitchen and I was working days for GKN selling building materials around the world and nights on Thrust 2. There was no internet and every letter had to be laboriously typed on my borrowed IBM Golfball typewriter and the copies were from carbon. Huge files of correspondence began to build up and just occasionally we would get the odd response; sometimes the responses were positive, but not very often.

We had a little money from our friends at Loctite, but the balance was reducing steadily. Our friends at Fulmen, who provided the batteries for Thrust 1, had pitched in.

From John's point of view, he must have had severe personal doubts about the whole programme. Here he was working long hours in a tiny kitchen and we couldn't even provide a landline – mobile phones were far in the future. His friends must have wondered about his obsession and the sudden adoption of an uncharacteristic hermit lifestyle.

First wind tunnel data, 1978.

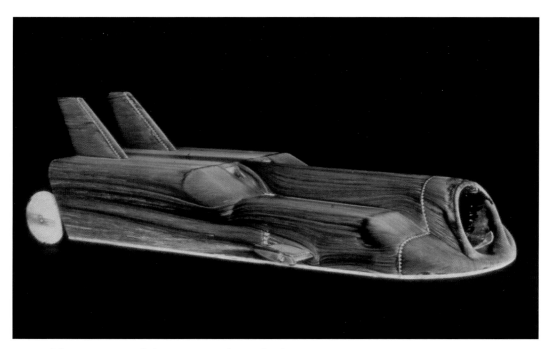

Oil flow test at British Aerospace wind tunnel, Filton, 1978.

But by September 1978 British Aerospace had run three weeks of low-speed wind tunnel testing on Thrust 2 and their opinion was that the car could take the record, but we would need to know much more abouts its transonic performance – as the design approaches the speed of sound (760 mph) the aerodynamic drag increases substantially and progressively.

John had thought it through and decided we needed to create the driving seat. The reasoning was good: we had achieved useful PR with the Motorfair stand and now we needed to show further progress. A cheap and obvious bit of car would do the job; the only trouble was there wasn't any car bits we could get the media excited with, so we had to make one.

The idea was simple: we would create my driving seat, set exactly to the conforms and shape of my body. After all, the car would accelerate at over 40 mph per second, so a good, comfortable, conforming seat would be essential. But more than that, the seat would be as nearly upright as we could make it. Under extreme acceleration I needed my body as near to vertical as possible, so that the blood would flow to my back and not away from my head. We didn't spend too much time on the deceleration, which would often exceed 5 g – that challenge would come later.

The idea was to create a large, wooden, liquid-tight, upright mould, which would include a floor-level base, the seat level at the backside and thighs and extending right up above my head. The mould box would have a clear poly sheet, which would separate me from the liquid polyurethane.

I have no idea how it happened, but the BBC *Tomorrow's World* team were interested in our struggles and decided they would like to film the experience.

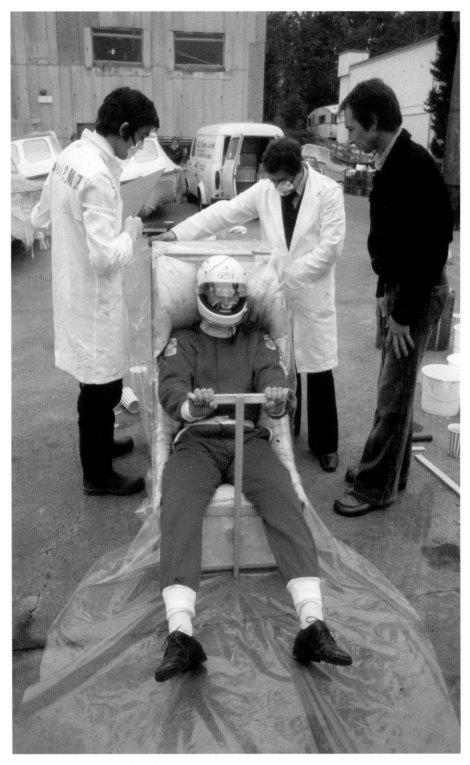

Moulding Richard Noble's Thrust 2 seat, 1978.

The great day came, and the weather was fine and hot. John's box was upright on the Ranalagh works dockside and a large BBC team arrived with cameras and microphone boom. Sitting in my old Thrust 1 racing suit with my Griffin helmet, I lowered myself cautiously into John's mould. Out of sight, John and his friends were quickly mixing up industrial quantities of liquid polyurethane, which would shortly react with an exothermic reaction. Using buckets, they poured the mixture into the box behind my head. Slowly, the polyurethane bubbled up as it morphed to foam, giving off heat, which gave me a warm and wet feeling.

15 minutes later the job was done, and we were into interview time. The BBC were pleased and I realised that I would have to maintain shape for the years ahead as the seat was a kind of negative statue.

The BBC aired the item a couple of weeks later, and they did a good job, which was just as well because Tony Waring, marketing manager at Initial Services, was watching.

The next stage was John Newble's TI Reynolds press conference to announce the start of building the frame. Part of the Birmingham factory had been cleared for Ken Sprayson and his supply of 531 tube, and Ken the welding maestro had a huge grin on his face. John and I brought up models to illustrate the case. John produced the most beautiful balsa model of the frame and I produced a rough model showing the famous twin fins and, of course, the British Airways logo on the fins. When screened by the BBC this caused a huge explosion at the British Airways Manchester office and a director had chased us down through the BBC network. He was on the phone: 'What do you think you are doing putting the British Airways logo on that model – we can take you to court over this!' It was important to remain cool in the face of threats: 'You see it really does work for you,' I said. 'What really does work for us?' I explained the remarkable British Airways deal we had just done and the man from Manchester wished us well and called off the dogs.

It really was a brilliant deal that made a huge contribution to the project at a time when we were desperately short of finance and wondering how we could maintain pace. If we had to stop, then we knew exactly what people would say and it would be unlikely to be helpful. We were on a tightrope, and could fall off so easily and there was a long way to fall.

A few months earlier I had banged out a proposal to British Airways on the trusted IBM Golfball. The gist of all this was simple: 'British Airways now has the Concorde – the world's fastest passenger plane, and to complete the unique set you need the world's fastest car.' For some reason the concept resonated and I found myself at the British Airways Cromwell Road, London, office with two very bright marketing executives.

'We have two problems,' they said. 'Firstly, the British Airways logo won't fit your supersonic tailfins.'

I called John: 'Tell them we'll use Boeing 747 tailfin co-ordinates,' he said. That seemed to settle them.

'The second point is that we haven't any money, but we want to do the deal.'

'OK,' I said. And gave them the normal response: 'We have a common problem. Have you got a printing press?'

This got the usual laugh, and they explained this is exactly what they had in mind. They weren't going to debase sterling, but they could generate funds for us.

They explained the amazing deal. Under the labyrinthine international airline operating agreements, the airline was allowed to refund used tickets and it was left to the airline to settle what was seen as small domestic arguments. 'All you need to do is to get us a supply of used British Airways tickets and we'll refund them.' I explained that I could supply a considerable supply of used tickets and it seemed there would be no cap on British Airways generosity.

Once back in the office I called my friends at GKN International, who spent their whole lives on international travel. They were disbelieving. 'All you have to do is travel with BA and send me the used ticket – we can then use that to build the car.'

The story ran around the huge GKN company like lighting and very soon large numbers of used tickets started to arrive. It wasn't long before other companies made contact to join in. John Ackroyd and Thrust were to be funded by used airline tickets – and this could go on for a very long time. We gave British Airways the tail fins and we had a real chance and a real future.

It was mid-year and John was in trouble. He was no longer alone on the project and he had to service growing numbers of engineers, suppliers and manufacturers who were interested or making parts – the project was coming alive. The TI Reynolds frame deal had driven the interest and John's workload was becoming impossible. He needed another designer.

An ad in the *Isle of Wight County Press* delivered Eddie Elsom, a fast-talking and very perceptive engineer dedicated to the Isle of Wight, but the relationship started off on the wrong foot. John was, as usual, working at breakneck pace with the knowledge that he knew exactly where he was going with the design – there was no way he could work with an understudy. Eddie called a halt to the failing relationship.

'John,' said Eddie, 'There is only ever going to be one designer for Thrust 2. I can't possibly draw what is in your head. What you need is an organiser to handle all the running around, so you can design the car.' John saw the sense in this immediately and Eddie became the Operations Manager and set about sorting what was becoming a huge project. About the same time John found a local secretary and his typing days were over.

While all this was going on, Ken Sprayson was coming to the end of his massive frame build and the TI directors wanted their corner of the factory back. Ken had forged ahead and kept his head down, but all around there were growing concerns about the project and TI Reynolds' involvement. Where is the big money coming from, they asked, aware that Donald Campbell's projects had involved huge sums. Who is the Noble bloke? What experience has he had to drive a project on this scale? Is TI Reynolds going to be dragged into a disaster when it all goes wrong? Should we quit now while we are ahead?

But John Newble was firmly in control. There was a solid media turnout with a very positive response. They were glad to see the huge space frame alongside the 20-foot Avon engine and afterburner from the upper installation on a Lightning. The frame would leave TI Reynolds that week and objectors would have to find other material to complain about.

Eddie Elsom – ace organiser and buyer.

The Avon engine fitted to the space frame, TI Reynolds, 1978.

The huge yellow frame was put on a truck with plenty of TI branding and driven down to London where it was parked opposite to my Twickenham home, causing yet more aggro from the couple across the road who claimed a god-given right to park outside their house.

The next move was to the island. Across on the ferry to Fishbourne, down the winding muddy track to Ranalagh (with help from a crane to lift the artic trailer), around the tight curves and into our new home, an open workshop shared with famous Isle of Wight aluminium race boat builder Ernie Simms.

John was appalled. The huge frame was finished in a poisonous yellow high-technology paint with a soft surface. 'It will take us all a month to get that back to bare metal and the air here is salt laden.' However, John had forgotten the Thrust Streamliners Supporters Club. The next weekend ten supporters got stuck in, and the paint was removed in one tempestuous day. 'I would never have believed it,' said John, as the project began to find its feet.

And coming with the frame was amazing master craftsman Ron Benton, with a brilliant sense of humour and who chose his projects very carefully. He had been a keen member of the famous pre-war Rudge Brooklands team and his home was full of pre-war racing bikes. He had worked on the *Queen Mary*, an early hovercraft; Britten-Norman Islanders; and John Britten and Des Norman prototype aircraft. Ron just sort of arrived and got started panelling up the huge frame, starting with the firewalls and driver's cockpit. We were hugely fortunate, but a quick look at the workshop explained everything. There was this huge workshop filled with a huge frame and its jet engine, and Ron Benton. It was clearly going to take a lifetime, and a lot more airline tickets, to get the car completed.

But before we got to that point we had to overcome another major problem. The Avon 210 needed fitting and the whole installation system required a wide range of special Lightning airframe parts. John and I found a friendly scrap dealer in Stafford with a de-winged Lightning in his yard and we agreed a price for a day's dismantling. We worked flat out until the gates closed and carried home a wide range of irreplaceable parts. The RAF came to our help and together with a group of highly motivated Streamliner supporters we were able to extract yet more parts from a dead Lightning used as an airfield decoy at RAF Coningsby. We had just about everything we needed and a great evening in the local pub after. It had been another hell of a long day.

While a great deal about the project was going right, we were about to run into trouble with British Airways. It was time to renew the contract. At this stage we were getting flooded with used tickets and clearly British Airways would have something to say. In fact, the tickets were piling up everywhere and if it went on like this we would be a line in British Airways' annual report.

The meeting date was arranged, and I turned up at the Cromwell Road offices, but the smart executives who had come up with the plan were elsewhere. I was summoned to meet the area manager in his big and special office a floor or so above.

I was surprised by his office – a large, imposing window and three walls lined with expensive black cork tiles. There were staged pictures of the manager shaking hands with famous classical conductors, who seemed pleased with British Airways largesse; but, strangely, there were no pictures or models of aircraft.

He opened with, 'Well, this is the last of the dangerous ones!' I asked for an explanation and reminded him that the promotion had been a great success – we were hitting the exact commercial traveller market they targeted. 'We are an airline and we can't afford to sponsor dangerous sports.' It wasn't helpful to remind him that this should have been considered before sign up – the man was determined and the lawyers would follow – and we hadn't enough tickets to fund a challenge.

'Ok so what is British Airways going to sponsor now that our relationship is over?' The manager was triumphant: 'British Airways is going to sponsor… orchestras!'

'In that case you will have to give me a couple of weeks.' 'Why should I? I have cancelled our arrangement,' he replied.

'It'll take me that time to get an orchestra together!' But there was no humour at British Airways, Cromwell Road, that day.

There seemed to be an amazing revolving door developing around Thrust, however. While British Airways were now out, a new sponsor had sought us out. Tony Waring, Marketing Manager of Initial Services, had been watching the BBC seat-moulding operation. He had an idea and he had travelled to the island to see the project.

Chapter 4
Island of Dreams

The arrival of Tony Waring provoked a much-needed sea of change at Project Thrust. Here was Initial Services, a would-be sponsor who had actually found us, rather than one who had responded to our enticing letters.

Tony Waring took his proposition to his director, Henry Lewis, and they decided to sponsor Thrust 2. Initial Services was a steady and successful business, but their products were challenging when it came to promotion. Their focus was on the provision and laundering of work overalls for the UK coal mines, power generation businesses and the provision of clever washroom furniture – highly profitable, but difficult to promote and excite public interest.

Waring had another objective, however. The laundry business at that time required repetitive manual loading and clearing washing machine contents on an industrial scale. Why not take on a massive international challenge to give the hardworking staff something to get excited about? It was an extraordinary move for a very traditional public limited company.

Initial Services – they made it all happen. (1979)

First there was an agreement to a £20,000 sponsorship – serious money at that stage of the project, and just in time. Back on the island the financial pressure was mounting. The car had to be designed, built in a certain sequence so the components fitted each other. It was important to move quickly, and the island's fast-moving, innovative and highly skilled supply chain came into its own.

John's productivity was prodigious and as each drawing was signed off, so the parts had to be made, and the project began to expand. I still remember the arrival of the Tube Investments chassis – there is a photo of the engine, the chassis and Ron Benton. It was only then that we began to realise the scale of what we were taking on. Ron Benton, alone in the workshop with this huge engine and space frame – how on earth do we get this finished? Around the same time the incredibly talented Gordon Flux joined us as Chief Engineer – a very hands-on role, responsible for all things

Ambition: Ron Benton and the space frame, 1979.

mechanical. Flux was a genius who could turn his hand to anything; he even invented a brilliant attachment for sailors that linked their safety harnesses to their sailing boat's rails and somehow enabled them to pass the stanchions without having to disconnect. None of us ever understood how it worked!

The cashflow was, of course, always a huge problem. Somehow we had to keep going and the sponsorship deals had to become larger, but the rate of increase of the sponsorships had to exceed the rate of increase in spend. The project was difficult to plan, so we planned by objectives. The next objective was to get the car, in space frame form, onto its wheels and then run it.

However, as the project grew, I was finding it tough going. It was no longer possible to keep pace with the project's demand. The old routine of starting at 5 a.m., going to my GKN office work at 8.30 a.m. and then continuing with Thrust after work was going to fail us because I couldn't keep the money coming in fast enough.

There was only one thing to do: write to GKN's chief executive, Roy Roberts, and explain. The CEO was some six layers of hierarchy management above me and I ended the letter with a suggestion that GKN should sponsor. The extraordinary thing about a letter like that is that it's like a bomb with a slow-burn fuse. I remember posting it in a red letter box in Ealing and then promptly forgot about it. Returning to the GKN office around ten days later, there was consternation in the office. The chief executive's response was on my desk. It said take eighteen months of paid leave of absence, make

John Ackroyd and his preferred transport.

Thrust 2 in build stages, Ranalagh, Isle of Wight, 1979.

Reheat fuel tank. (1979)

sure that the GKN brand was on the car, and go and get the world record. I cleared my desk and left within the hour.

At this stage in the story we need to understand exactly the challenges facing the design team. The previous British land speed record projects had finished back in 1964 with Donald Campbell's CN7 wheel-driven car, which had achieved a record of 403 mph. The Thrust 2 team were aiming at a peak speed of 650 mph – an increase of 247 mph, or 61 per cent. It's no wonder the British public were sceptical. The general view was that a pencil-thin rocket car was needed, like the Blue Flame of 1970.

But John Ackroyd believed otherwise. Much later, the Thrust 2 design would be tested in the British Aerospace Byfleet transonic tunnel and amazed the professionals who would prepare a detailed analysis. They confirmed the car could be expected to achieve 650 mph.

Of course, a land speed record car has to be designed in conjunction with the track on which it will operate. The team's view was that since the Blue Flame had taken the record on Bonneville Salt Flats in Utah, USA, then that was the ideal track – we knew no other. On a good year Bonneville would provide 11 miles of rock-hard salt, but while the Blue Flame had high-pressure Goodyear tyres, Thrust 2 would use high-speed, solid, aluminium wheels – a solution that seemed obvious since no manufacturer showed interest in risking design and manufacture of 650 mph tyres. We had a lot to learn.

The best way to understand the Thrust 2 design was to review previous accidents and try and do better. Other than mechanical accidents, there were two classes of aero-stability accidents: the ones where the car would pitch nose up and fly, and the more common class where the car would diverge off the course and turn sideways. We were to experience plenty of that on Bonneville.

So, to deal with the first case, it was important to design as much weight as possible into the front of the car, so that at least 60 per cent of the car's overall weight was on the front wheels. Here the 25-foot-long Rolls-Royce Avon 302, weighing 3,700 lbs, works in our favour: the heavy section is the forward compressor combustion and turbine section, while the all-important afterburner is by comparison a lightweight tube. So the car has to have a forward centre of gravity – the point where the whole car would balance. Another important point is that the fuel content of the car (124 gallons in the case of Thrust 2) should be positioned behind the centre of gravity, so as the weight of the fuel reduces as it is burned the centre of gravity moves ever so slightly forwards.

The second case is more complex. To minimise aero drag the car should be long and thin as the drag is proportional to the maximum cross-sectional aero of the car. But the longer the car is, the more sensitive it might be to diverging – known as stability in yaw. A small yaw divergence (turn) will of course expose more of the forward side of the car to the onward airflow and cause an increase in a diverging force trying to drive the front of the car to one side. As the car responds to this forward lateral force, it may try to yaw even further, and there comes a point when whatever the driver does by applying opposite steering to try to recover the straight line, recovery becomes impossible. The car diverges sideways on. The high-velocity airflow will divert to flowing diagonally across the top of the car, causing very considerable lift, and the car will fly. It's important to understand that these aero forces increase as the square of the speed go twice as fast and the aero force can increase by a factor of four.

So, what is required is an aero design that naturally goes straight. An arrow or dart is the ideal example, having as much weight as desirable at the front and a long, thin body with the feathers at the back. The longer the body (the further back the feathers are), the more directionally stable the car will tend to be. There are of course opposing considerations. As an example, the jet engine (which in Thrust 2's case came from upper engine installation of a Mach 2 Lightning fighter) was the result of many hours of the manufacturer's incredibly expensive engine optimisation. Since the supersonic exhaust flow from the reheated engine would be likely to destroy any lightweight bodywork in proximity to the exhaust duct nozzle, the length of the engine would define the length of the car. John Ackroyd came up with an unusual solution to increasing the directional stability of the car: he decided to design two tail fins, which would increase the directional stability without raising the fin centre of pressure, which would happen if the car just had one large fin, thus reducing the rolling moment that would come with a large single fin. This decision was to pay big dividends.

Of course, we have to discuss the stability in roll – the threat of the car rolling over sideways at speed. Some land speed record cars have tended to be quite tall and given a high-speed divergence in yaw the cars could more easily roll. Thrust 2 was very wide and low with a low centre of gravity; this saved the car when we had to make a 200-mph sharp left turn to save the car during the Greenham Common accident in June 1982. One might argue that designers should try to make future land speed record cars low and wide rather than to narrow and tall.

What we have been discussing is known as primary safety – trying to make the experimental car as safe as we can so that the car doesn't have a dynamic accident. Apart from all the engineering there is one key point: we need to ensure that the car can be recovered if it starts to diverge. It sounds simple, but it isn't. The driver has to be able to see where they are going and has to be able to feel the car – just like a light aircraft pilot can feel how the aircraft is performing. So the driver has to sit as near as possible to the centre of gravity.

So, the car featured a safety seat, moulded to the driver's body, with a six-point harness to prevent submarining where, in the case of high g-force deceleration, the driver could slip downwards and forwards through the harness. Arms and wrists are of course important, so the wrists are shackled to the harness, allowing just enough movement to drive the car. The driver's suit is made from an incredible fireproof material – Panotex – with appropriate fireproof underwear and fighter pilot's leather gloves and boots. Rubber overshoes were important to prevent dust or salt being carried into the cockpit when first climbing in. The cockpit has to be very clean and dust free.

There could be problems with cockpit air in the event of a cockpit seal failure or dust incursion, in which case the driver has to have a sensible air supply with a dedicated bottle. Not oxygen, which could induce a driver 'high' and all kinds of problems, but ordinary compressed air with a diver's regulator.

Wheels and suspension represent an opportunity for sensible innovation. Although GoodYear claimed to have made rubber tyres with an 850 mph capability, it was common sense to try to progress to solid, aluminium, cart-type wheels, which would be safe at 700 mph – that's 8,000 rpm just within the safe capability of aluminium alloy. An advantage of the solid wheel is that the wheel can be designed to fit the car, not the car to fit the wheel. Once we had the wheel design correct we found that they almost never needed changing, unlike a rubber tyre, which would be changed for safety after every high-speed run. Rubber aircraft tyres would be used for low-speed aircraft runway runs and for car short distance positioning.

This then leads to the all-important design of the suspension. The car is going to peak at 650 mph and every little bump is likely to have an effect on the suspension – for instance where there may be a slight hollow in the ground, the car could fly across the cavity. John's double wishbone front suspension and trailing arm rear suspension together with the wheels and brakes would be achieved for an unsprung weight of just 9 per cent. The suspension has to control the car in pitch and very small movements were preferred, so we decided to use a special Aeon rubber suspension system, which would allow small movements of the order of 1 inch with the spring rate increasing substantially with small deflection. The rubber mix had to be specially made for us by the Malaysian Rubber Manufacturers Research Association, and it was a huge success.

The steering ratio was 25:1 (25 degrees input at the steering wheel would give 1 degree at the front wheels), which meant that in practice the car could be positioned

Rear suspension. (1979)

with an accuracy of 40 mm at 650 mph and with the driver making constant trimming inputs of the order for 45 degrees at the steering wheel.

Stopping is of course obligatory, and John calculated that at 650 mph Thrust 2 would roll brakeless for 8.5 miles. Of course, every effort to reduce the car aero drag would adversely affect the braking. The primary braking is by the 7-foot, 6-inch-diameter military supersonic chutes, which were designed to be deployed at 650 mph with a retarding for of 22,000 lbs. A secondary triple-chute system could be deployed at 375 mph if emergency braking were required at this lower speed, where the primary system was less effective. The triple-chute system was seldom used, and for UK runway development runs different chutes were used in order to preserve the high-speed canopies. The best runway chute was the GQ 14-foot ribbon chute, which gave sterling service. The canopies are deployed with 20 feet of 32-mm nylon rope, which can provide an extension of 20 per cent and de-shock both car and driver.

The secondary braking was of course by the wheel brakes. This was the work of Lucas Girling engineer Glynne Bowsher, and represented a considerable challenge. Of course, the wheel brake discs had to survive the stresses of 8,000 rpm rotation, though we could never apply the wheel brakes above 200 mph as the huge energy would simply burn out and destroy the discs, pads and most probably the wheels as well. To enable the discs to survive the stresses of max speed, Glynne specified a special Bainitic iron mix and they were each balanced and spin tested to 720 mph before fitting. In practice the wheel discs survived multiple runs over 600 mph and a peripheral velocity of 525 feet per second –twice the bursting speed of a traditional cast-iron flywheel. The wheel brakes were power assisted from a hydraulic feed from the engine and, later, an electric-driven pump to maintain pressure without engine pre-rotation.

What we were building was an engineering masterpiece, all thought through and designed from reading books and watching films and videos. We had never stood on the Bonneville Salt Flats – we didn't have the time or funds to travel in those early days. It was probably just as well because we were creating a radically different design and time spent on the salt might have diluted the purity of the original thinking.

Chapter 5
Time to Get Moving

John had a sensible plan: get the car onto its wheels in space frame form and build team experience in operating it. The expensive bodywork could come later. What was needed was operational experience, both for the rookie driver and the entire operational team. The car was put on its Leyland transporter and showed for the first time at the Tower Hotel in central London. The initial PR team, realising the photogenic limitations of the hairy engineers, thoughtfully provided a beautiful model in a Thrust T-shirt to front the photos, in true 1980s motor show style.

This was followed by an incredible turn of events. The project was running out of money and out of new sponsors. We held a financial sponsors meeting in London

The first media showing Thrust 2 on wheels, Tower Hotel, London, 1980.

and it was clear that the project was moving outside of the current sponsors' comfort zone. They made the point that they had joined to give to the project a solid start in life, but now that the programme was underway and expanding they found themselves in difficulty. There was to be a little more cash. We left the meeting with a sinking feeling – all that huge effort in winning the sponsors was lost, and just when we had the car on its wheels. We had no further immediate financial prospects.

I took a call from Richard Chisnell at Initial. Tony Waring had been back to the board and they had decided to double up their sponsorship; the funds were immediate and we could continue. While the episode made it clear that we had solid support from our friends at Initial, it also reminded us just how financially vulnerable the project was. We were driving a no-reserves project. If we slowed up then the project would take too long and the team and sponsors would lose interest. We had to keep running it as fast as it would go. The importance of the project's speed of delivery was paramount – we had to continually amaze our audiences.

The next moves were critical. With ex-RAF specialists Tony Meston and Geoff Smee in charge, we took the car to RAF Coningsby where, tied down in the engine test pan, we ran the engine up to full power and then lit the afterburner with its 30-foot flame accompanied by massive thunder. The noise and flame were truly awesome close up and we wondered how this enormous power we had talked so glibly about to the

First Avon 210 reheat run, RAF Coningsby, 1980.

public and sponsors was going to affect the car's performance and stability. We were to learn very soon.

Of course, we needed to run the car on a runway somewhere – but where? As soon as we mentioned the afterburner the airports immediately lost interest. Every airport has its noise problem and locals who have to be calmed with careful mitigation, but to bring in Thrust 2 would shake up the locality with a thunder and unwind many years of patient mitigation at a stroke. It wasn't going to happen.

But Colonel Pat Reger had a different view. The Army School of Mechanical Transport had its operational base at the old RAF Lightning airfield at Leconfield, near Hull. The airfield was being used for driver training and the runway was repurposed with traffic lights and typical road signage. Even worse, the runway featured a large rise in the middle, which meant it was impossible to see the far end or even judge your stopping distance.

But this was our sole chance, so we went for it. At the first run with the engine on cold power, Tony Meston accompanied the car on his motorcycle. He wasn't impressed with a first drive of 50 mph. Ever so slowly, we built confidence and speed, but the inability see the far end of the runway and the huge implications of using the afterburner for the first time began to sap the team's confidence. They anticipated a much better performance and faster development, and they didn't get it.

It came a few days later, however, when we were doing a development run at the Royal Naval Air Station at HMS *Daedalus* at an air show preview, when the whole

John Ackroyd's passenger ride at the first trials, Leconfield, 1980.

Above and below: The best runways and 200 mph passes were found on the UK air show circuit. (1980)

show came together and Thrust 2 hared down the runway with full afterburner and a 200-mph pass.

For the rest of the summer of 1980, we were running the skeleton of Thrust 2, making over 200-mph passes with massive noise and public acclaim. The plan of integration with the air show circuit was a real winner, building driver and car experience on the best runways in the country.

So as a team we now had experience and a lot of media coverage, but no real credibility. By sheer good fortune we discovered a little-known agreement signed in Downing Street that allowed the occasional use of the US Greenham Common nuclear airbase runway for worthwhile amateur development. We appeared to qualify, and in September 1980 we set about timed runs and record-breaking for the first time. The Cold War runway was 10,000 feet (1.9 miles) long. The RAC were doing the sanctioning and timing.

There was no way that our heavy jet car designed to withstand huge aerodynamic loads at over 600 mph could be compared to a traditional dragster, but we could give it a very good try and we had the ideal GQ 14-foot-diameter braking parachute, which meant that we could stop incredibly quickly

Trying to maintain speed with two passes over a timed mile was to prove challenging on such a short runway and we would complete the back-to-back runs with the car using almost the entire length of the runway. We also had to bear in mind that Dunlop had rated the car's Lightning tyres at just 260 mph, so our speeds were limited.

British land speed record: setting up ident, 1980.

Thrust 2 at RAF Greenham Common, 1980.

The start of UK record runs, RAF Greenham Common, 1980.

In two days of record-breaking over 24 and 25 September 1980, we found ourselves with six national speed records, including the famous flying mile at 248.87 mph, being the average of the speeds over two passes within the hour. This was commonly known as the British land speed record, and we held it. But not without risk and difficulty. The runway was 1.9 miles long and so we had only 0.45 miles for acceleration and 0.45 miles for stopping, which of course is obligatory. At one end of the runway we had a deep quarry – a serious risk. So this was exact, high-speed driving, the most important element of which was the exact deployment of the brake parachute at the end of the mile: too early and it would affect our average speed; too late and we would be in the quarry. Usually, we would stop with violent braking 12 feet from the end of the tarmac.

All the car prep was in the capable hands of Chief Engineer Gordy Flux, who had an uncanny feel for almost all the operation.

John Ackroyd was concerned about tyre skid marks on the concrete: 'Richard you must be applying the wheel brakes at the end of the mile?'

'I am not, John. I don't start braking until we are well below 200 mph.'

John was at a loss to explain the skid marks until Gordy explained it: 'As soon as that huge GQ brake parachute is deployed the deceleration is so violent that the rear wheels, with all that inertia, can't slow down fast enough and wheels are spinning.' This was the first time anyone had heard of wheelspin while braking.

Correct deployment of the brake parachute, 1980.

Gordy Flux, the chief mechanic.

The records are hard won and worth recording:

1 mile standing start	166.47 mph
1 kilometre standing start	149.57 mph
Flying quarter mile	259,74 mph
Flying 500 metres	255.06 mph
Flying kilometre	251.19 mph
Flying mile	248.87 mph

The next stage had to be the world land speed record, with 11 miles on the Bonneville Salt Flats in Utah, US, in perfect hard conditions. With the car completed, with its new aerodynamic bodywork and 700-mph solid tyreless wheels, we ought to knock this off easily, or so we thought. We were very, *very* wrong...

Chapter 6
Bonneville Salt Flats, Utah

The project team were in high spirits. We now held the British land speed record and, following the summer's air show campaign, the project's car and team had considerable media exposure and there was growing public interest. There was still talk about Thrust 2 being the wrong shape for a world record but, knowing John's careful analyses, the team and sponsors kept up the pressure.

But I had a concern that had been worrying me for the last year. A few years before I had been privileged to spend an evening with Leo Villa, who had been chief engineer for both Sir Malcolm and Donald Campbell. Leo had a great friendship with Donald Campbell, whom he had known since a boy, and he was present on Coniston when the K7 Bluebird had taken off at 300 mph, resulting in the terrible accident. We met at Leo and Joan's home in Reigate, started talking at 7 p.m. and by 3 a.m. I was exhausted, but Leo was still going. This was a truly wonderful opportunity to learn first-hand.

There was one crucial point that Leo kept on labouring: 'You never have enough engine power.' What he was trying to say was that despite the best efforts of the designers, the aero drag and the wheel rolling resistance often turn out to be much greater than predicted, so much more engine power is needed.

The RAF had a similar problem with the Lightning fighters. While Thrust 2 was powered with an Avon 210 engine and the afterburner from a Lightning F1, the RAF and Rolls-Royce had moved up a notch with the new Rolls-Royce Avon variant: the 302, which gave 17,000 lbs of thrust but is physically longer and needs a different afterburner and fuel pumping arrangement with the fueldraulic afterburner pump. This would mean changes to Thrust 2 and the time to do it would be right now – before the beautiful handmade aluminium bodywork was shaped and fitted.

The changes were substantial and not popular, but in the years to come they would save the project. Leo was right: we needed much more power than we planned.

Back at Fishbourne the team swung into action to complete Thrust 2. The standards were very high, and the workload massive. Even the Rolls-Royce Avon 302, which usually has an isopropyl nitrate (AVPIN) starter system, had to be modified to take the airstart unit, which had proved so successful in 1980. There was good reason: in the F 6 Lightning pilot notes it makes it clear that if the Avpin starter fails the Avon start for any reason the aircraft has to be abandoned for 60 minutes to allow the volatile starter gasses to disperse.

Ron Benton, Gordy Flux, Brian Ball and Mike Barrett took on the enormous and painstaking job of completing the bodywork. Every section had to be handmade, and every section included the perfect under structure, which enabled the carefully shaped sheets to fit precisely. The way John Ackroyd had designed the car, he had tried to minimise double curvature of the aluminium sheet. Aluminium bends easily in one direction, but at the front of Thrust 2 and over the cockpits there are double curvature sections. To make these complex sections requires the use of an English wheel – a large, floor-standing unit with two vertical, touching, precision wheels clamped in its jaws. The aluminium sheet is carefully fed and reversed between the tight wheels, which stretches it on one face and induces a curve. The curve has to be continuously checked against the horse (an exact wooden tool that defines the panel shape). The genius behind all this was Brian Ball, the man who single-handedly made the huge tailplane bullets on the VC 10 airliners. Brian had been encouraged to make the trip from British Aerospace at Hurn Airport by his friend Norman Willis, and after that he spent much of his next years with the project. The perfect bodywork was to be a real marvel of workmanship and is much admired today, over forty years later.

One outcome from the new British land speed record was that British Aerospace decided to investigate the car's potential transonic performance using the transonic tunnel at British Aerospace Byfleet. The idea was to find out just how fast the car would go with the Avon 302 engine. As a jet fighter accelerates towards the speed of sound (760 mph), the aircraft itself may be still subsonic, but airflow, which is accelerated over curved sections of the fuselage and wings, may go supersonic first. This speed zone is known as the transonic speed range, which is ranged between 80 per cent and

Brian Ball, master of the English wheel.

120 per cent of the speed of sound. As the airflow locally goes supersonic the shock waves develop and sap power; consequently, a hefty increase in engine power is needed to keep accelerating. The question was whether the Avon 302 would generate enough power to drive Thrust 2 so deep into the transonic speed zone.

A critical point was the first fitting of the intake, which was a huge event and for the first time gave us the final full size and shape of the car.

When John and the beautiful 1/30th transonic test model arrived at Byfleet the British Aerospace aerodynamicists were dismayed. They thought a much slimmer model would be needed. They didn't like the almost blunt front and the cockpit position, which was replicated on the left side. There was negative talk and they seemed to think the whole programme was a waste of time. So, it was a big surprise when they rang John with the test results. 'We have no idea why,' they said, 'but it seems to be really good. Depending on temperature and other considerations, we believe the car could make 650 mph.'

Thrust 2 had a fair chance of peaking at 650 mph and raising the existing world record of 622 mph. John had got it right from the very start. There was now no immediate need of a next generation car; we were to go for the world record with Thrust 2 and the sponsors now had authoritative confirmation. Now we had to plan for Bonneville in 1981 and the world land speed record.

Arguing with the Bonneville season is like trying to control the tides. The huge salt lake is at 4,000 feet above sea level and can be expected to be dry in August and September, and sometimes in October. But as the winter comes to the Sierra Nevada

Fitting the intake, 1980.

The real proof: Thrust 2 transonic wind tunnel model.

mountains it starts to rain and Bonneville becomes a massive cold water lake. And it will stay that way until the next year's summer provides enough heat to dry off the water. Timing and planning are crucial.

The Thrust 2 programme now had to get the car finished and painted, then attend a major public launch at the NEC with our sponsors Initial, and finally be strapped to its large blue wooden pallet and delivered to Heathrow for the flight to Los Angeles.

The car was rolled out in its beautiful aluminium form and the sheer workmanship had to be seen to be believed. It seems a shame to paint it – but we have sponsors to look after and the desert track at Bonneville is corroding salt. The paint was beautifully applied by Eric White's team in Ascot. There was a bit of problem because perfectionist Ron Benton was still working on the driver's side overnight and was running the risk of being painted in!

The Thrust launch was superbly handled by Initial, who were also using the set for their annual customer conference. The good will in the audience was amazing and for the fun of it we had a sponsorship auction, selling off a small patch of unsold advertising real estate on Thrust 2. This went down well and made a valuable last-minute addition to our funds.

Thrust 2 had to be flown because not only would shipping take too long and lose us valuable preparation time, but also the constant ship vibration would brinell the critical engine bearings. The arrangement had to be made with the famous Flying Tigers cargo airline with the all-important 747 nose loading arrangement. The transporter and trucks had to be sent off by sea much earlier, so without tools and a workshop the Isle of Wight team had a valuable break.

Left: Thrust rollout unpainted, 1981.

Below: Thrust 2 painted at Eric White's garage in Reading, 1981.

Thrust at the Initial Services launch event, 1981.

Loading Thrust 2, Heathrow, 1983.

1O DOWNING STREET

THE PRIME MINISTER

24th September 1981

Dear Mr. Noble,

It is with great pleasure that I have learned of project Thrust and of your plans to try to break the World Land Speed Record next month on the Salt Flats at Utah.

Britain has a proud history of holding World Speed Records on land, sea and air. I would like to congratulate you and your small team on the enthusiasm and determination which over recent years has carried you so far, and which last year resulted in your breaking the British Land Speed Record.

I hope the weather conditions in Utah will be favourable for a successful two-way run, and I wish you every success.

All good wishes.

Yours sincerely

Margaret Thatcher

Richard Noble Esq

Letter from Prime Minister Margaret Thatcher, 1981.

Just before we all left the UK we were surprised to receive a charming and unexpected letter from the British prime minister, Margaret Thatcher, which was hugely welcome.

But where did the money ultimately come from? Thrust 2 was always strapped for cash and with the car complete the choices were bleak: either go to Bonneville and try for the world record or give up the battle and put the car in a museum as yet another example of a British project with so much expectation that was forced into premature failure by financial realities. The day was saved by Mike Kemp, the *Daily Mail* motoring journalist who came up with Trust Securities, a highly ambitious property developer with an incredible site near Heathrow. There is an amazing story to come about Trust Securities, but this comes later.

But while we are on the subject we ought to talk about pluvious insurance. If you are running a weather risk and putting together an outdoor event in Britain, like a fête, you can generally take out pluvious insurance to insure/recover losses caused by unexpected weather. Given the uncertainties of Bonneville weather and our huge travel and operational costs we set out to get a deal. In return for our last £1,000, we could insure £75,000 of costs against the event being wrecked by weather. There will be more on this later too.

Travel was a real expedition. The plan was to ship the trucks and transporter via the Vestey Blue Star Line to Los Angeles, collect Thrust 2 from the airport and then drive the 600 miles over the mountains to Wendover, Utah. A huge, wooden, air portable pallet had to be made for Thrust 2 and it would only fit in a nose-loading B747.

Thrust 2 on the Bonneville Salt Flats, 1981.

Setting up the Thrust 2 base on Bonneville, 1981. Note the orange Palouste jet starters.

Thrust 2 starts its first 400-mph run at Bonneville, 1981.

Magically, the entire team turned up on time at Bonneville. Our base camp was built on the famous salt flats and Thrust 2 was unrolled from its trailer – all the way from the Isle of Wight and onto the famous Bonneville salt. It was an amazing team achievement to have even got the car and everyone to the famous lunar-style landscape. We were all fired up; after all, we held the British land speed record and we only had another 400 mph to claim the world record. We had enormous power in hand. It all seemed so obvious at the time.

But this time we were no longer on our Dunlop tyres; we were on John Ackroyd's solid aluminium wheels for the first time. Everyone expected an easy transition. It wasn't.

The Bonneville racers had tried solid wheels and even high-speed caterpillar tracks with mixed results. In the absence of help, John had chosen a 4-inch-wide tread for the front 30-inch wheels, which carry more than 50 per cent of the car's weight.

It was time for the first run. The pleasure of being behind the Thrust 2's steering wheel again was quickly forgotten. As I was being towed to the start line I wondered whether the steering was even connected. Whatever input I put in the car only gradually, and reluctantly, responded. Gone was Thrust 2's precise and accurate steering. There was no way I could take any emergency action with such indecisive steering. In fact, the car was now close to being very dangerous. This is always difficult to explain to the team, and even the more so if you are a rookie driver.

We made the first run on our special Bonneville track and the car drifted off to the right, leaving the track at 90 mph.

Thrust 2 on Bonneville Salt Flats in 1981, suffering a loss of directional control at 175 mph.

We tried again the next day and left the track at 175 mph, going 2 miles into the desert. A day or so later we were near sideways at 250 mph. We had an unresponsive car with a mind of its own and, although John made multiple changes, there was no improvement and we had to push on with a car we no longer understood. The prospect of a high-speed departure putting the car sideways meant a really serious airborne accident – a repeat of the one that had nearly killed Donald Campbell in 1964.

The lack of progress was destroying our happy and ambitious team. Simply put, either the car or the driver was at fault and after the huge engineering effort it was unthinkable that the car could be the cause.

As the runs persisted the solid wheels dug into the salt and the track became reminiscent of the railway tracks leading to Waterloo station, which made life even more difficult. Gradually, the speed increased as confidence returned, but each run was dicey, requiring minimal steering inputs. I was not using the afterburner since I reckoned this would destabilise an already directionally unstable car. John joined me in the port cockpit for at attempt on 400 mph. We took a long, long run in and finally saw 400 mph on the instruments. John said he wasn't going to experience that again.

The next day we decided we would try a record attempt turnaround – a test for trial land speed record run, albeit at just 400 mph. The first run was a vanilla 392 mph run, dodging through the ruts and railway like points on the worn-out course. The all-important 50-minute turnaround was a shambles: one vehicle broke its propshaft and to try and save the day the car was towed by our accountant, David Brinn, who was never first choice for the role.

Angry at our constant failures, I banged the car into full afterburner and the car ran as straight as a die, leaving the team whooping and cheering at the sudden change of fortune. Thrust 2 and I raced steadily up to 500 mph. Then, due to all the banging and jarring on the rough desert, the car battery came lose, the fuel pump died and we lost speed in the precious measured mile. The timekeepers gave us 447 mph for the second run and a 418 mph average. Now for the first time we were the fastest ever British car and driver. But I had seen 500 mph on the speedo and I knew we could hack this. There was a smile of relief on John Ackroyd's face – it had been a very difficult time for all of us.

That night it rained and there was a massive electrical storm. We spent the night hanging onto the workshop tent, which threatened to fly and take Thrust 2 with it.

The next morning Bonneville had returned to its a natural form – a beautiful 3-inch-deep reflective lake. It was obviously time to go home, but we did have the official timekeeper's slip – the only proof we had that we had achieved something. But now we knew how to handle the car and we had just over 130 mph to go.

But there was a lot to look forward to. The team had finally come together well and there were the battles of 1982 to look forward to, and that included the pluvious insurance…

Right: Designer John Ackroyd.

Below: The famous 1981 return. An average 447–500 mph was seen on the cockpit instruments.

400 mph Thrust 2 wheel tracks, Bonneville, 1981.

It's over! Time to go home. Bonneville floods again. (1981)

Fortunately, we had taken the team photo the day before.

Chapter 7

What on Earth is Happening to Us?

Flying Tigers delivered Thrust 2 back to us at Heathrow on 19 October 1981. We were out of money and we needed an urgent refuel. Mike Barrett kindly took the car to Earl's Court Motor Show, where a space had been made available. This was a highly successful two weeks, resulting in an immediate request to rent the car for the Jochen Rindt motor show in Essen in December. It also gave Mike and the team the opportunity to experience the huge levels of public interest in what we had achieved.

Our sponsors at Faberge were not thrilled: 'You promised us gold and you delivered silver!' It was difficult to explain to UK-bound sponsors just how difficult the project was and that 500 mph wasn't a bad achievement for the first outing for the team.

All this promotional activity was not popular with John. The Bonneville salt spray from the front wheels had liquidised with the wheel energy and flowed back along the car. The liquid salt had found its way into every crevice on the bodywork and between the aluminium panels. Despite everyone's efforts at car washing, the remaining salt solution reverted to crystals and the huge energy involved began to separate panels and spring rivets. Any parts that were steel began to corrode badly – the suspension units looked a real mess. John's beautiful car was beginning to look like a barn find.

But we needed the money, so while Terry Hopkins (our truck driver), Eddie Elsom and Mike Barrett set off for Essen we began the big fight to claim our insurance payback. The insurance companies regularly write pluvious insurance policies that are typically there to offset losses to outdoor events like fêtes and agricultural shows where rain can destroy the event and the cashflow. Somehow we had managed to insure Bonneville against rain during our event. The Utah locals will tell you that Bonneville always floods every year when the snow comes to the Sierra Nevada mountains; it's just a matter of when.

Not only did we have the pluvious policy, but the insurance company, understanding that they were insuring a desert against rain, had given us a 75:1 policy. We had given them our last £1,000 and, having been washed out, we expected £75,000 in return. After all, film of our team's efforts and the Bonneville flood had been shown on the BBC's *Tomorrow's World*, so there was no shortage of evidence.

Dealing with the insurance company was like a gigantic chess game, which we had to win – everybody's work and commitment was on the line. The insurance company told us they would appoint an assessor. We asked who paid the assessor and they said that they did. We called bias and said we would not accept the assessor's ruling unless the assessor was independently funded.

As expected, the assessor found there was no claim. Their case was that they had insured a record attempt and because we had only got to 440 mph for the mile, a long way away from 630 mph, there was no record attempt. We explained that the whole activity was a record attempt. We had the USAC timekeepers on site for the whole period, and a record attempt is defined as the work up to record speeds.

The next move was fascinating. We called a meeting of the financial sponsors to review progress and forward plans and invited the insurance company's director to explain his company's position to the sponsors. I confirmed that we had called a London press conference for two weeks hence and there was a very good response.

'You should have told us that!' The insurance company director sensed a loss of situational control.

'No. This is a matter for the project's sponsors, and you are not a sponsor.'

'What are you going to tell the media?' I explained that depended on the insurance company. If they decided to pay up we would praise them to the ends of the earth. If they decided not to pay, we would hand out copies of the policy to the journalists.

'You wouldn't do that!'

The insurance man was losing the plot. I explained that we have a duty to our team and sponsors, so please understand that we certainly would. There was no further communication from the insurance company. The press conference was very well attended and ably moderated by TV *World of Sports* anchor Dickie Davies. The insurance director appeared with a cheque for £75,000 in a special grey leather folder. The project was to go to the next stage, and this time the sponsors would take out the pluvious insurance.

After success with the insurance and the press conference, I went round to the financial sponsors to obtain their support for the 1982 campaign. They were all incredibly supportive, but I left visiting Trust Securities until last – the reason being that what we had already received was a generous once-off donation that I didn't expect them to repeat.

Trust Securities were a bit miffed that I had approached them last, and they wanted to share their amazing news. It seems that under competitive pressure Trust had bought a site in Manchester that had almost no access. In fact, the only possible site access was by buying up and demolishing a local worthy's home. Trust discovered too late that the owner had made it clear he would not sell under any circumstances. Faced with imminent disaster the Trust negotiators arrived at the householder's door for the meeting.

'Who are you?' they were asked. They explained, and there was a long silence. 'Are you anything to do with the Thrust land speed record team?'

By a million-to-one chance, the Trust executives had found themselves negotiating with a land speed record afficionado. The deal was done. Trust explained that the Thrust sponsorship had saved them from a very difficult situation and they spontaneously made the commitment to sponsor the project until it completed.

After, Essen John and the team had Thrust 2 back and set about a major rebuild. The salt damage was considerable and recovery required a total strip down and repaint or replating. A considerable amount of work went on the underside of the car, which had to be stiffened – an unpleasant job requiring Mike Barrett to spend weeks on his back under the car working the aluminium and generating swarf and filings, which would get in his eyes, nose and overalls.

Another key change was the addition of driver's armrests. Driving Thrust 2 at speed on tarmac was straightforward, but on salt Thrust 2 behaved like a rally car, so to ensure absolute accuracy of control the driver's elbows had to be firmly positioned on the new armrests. The ride was rough and the elbows were vigorously on the move. This change made a considerable improvement. We also needed to soften the headrest surface, as the vibration from the rough ride on the salt was affecting driver's vision. The battery also needed a more secure mount.

There was also a much more important change: I had found that the combination of managing the project and driving the car required a very heavy workload and super-high, continuous personal stress. So, we invited Ken Norris to join us as team leader on the desert, and much of the team's success was due to Ken's quiet, considered and thoughtful desert management. Ken's extensive background included the design of Donald Campbell's K7 Bluebird water speed record boat and the 400 mph Bluebird CN-7 land speed record car. Despite all of Ken's extensive experience with the Bluebird operations he almost never mentioned them, which was greatly appreciated by the team as he was devoting his time and energy to Thrust and the present. And shortly we were to need his help, big time.

The date 16 June 1981 saw us doing test runs again at Greenham Common, but this time as a press day. All went well with the 220-mph runs. I was aware I was short of Thrust 2 practice so asked John for one further run before we packed up and went home. John was reluctant as he had just signed off the car for the 1982 return to Bonneville, but he eventually agreed.

The run was to be another routine run, a repeat of the earlier one. We were to accelerate in max burner and cancel the afterburner and engine when we were alongside our red Jaguar Firechase recovery car. Careful positioning of the Jaguar would coincide with 220 mph. In fact, the only difference on this run was that Mike Barrett, our parachute specialist, was to occupy the passenger seat, so he could experience parachute deployment. We were using second-grade aircraft braking parachutes to save our special chutes.

The run was a frightening experience. We accelerated down the runway and I missed the red Jaguar and just kept going. The car reached over 300 mph. The parachute failed and using the last resort – wheelbrakes – we locked wheels and skidded for 4,000 feet before turning left onto the peritrack at 200 mph to avoid going off the end of the runway and into a quarry. The front of the Thrust 2 was extensively damaged. Stones

Above, below and overleaf: Thrust 2's 300-mph crash at RAF Greenham Common, 1982.

and grass had been hoovered up by the precious engine, but John's design had saved mine and Mike's lives. Amazingly, neither of us were injured. We were incredibly lucky.

The team were shattered by the disaster, and we lost John for a week; some thought he was very close to leaving the project. Ken chaired the team enquiry and John plotted the performance curve, but I couldn't account for my failure to see the red Jaguar. John's report stated that the accident 'was directly attributed to lack of discipline of both driver and team', which I felt was unfair – the accident had been caused by my personal failure, not the team's. We decided that we would all continue the programme and that I had to improve personal discipline and gain my IMC pilot's rating – a very demanding challenge requiring considerable textbook learning and endless instrument flying in cloud.

The damaged Avon engine was a massive problem. The accident had cost us our goodwill and securing a replacement seemed impossible. No one wanted to help.

John Watkins, our RAF engine specialist (known as 'One Take' because of his legendary ability to run off complex TV interviews in one pass), called for the engine to be sent up to his engine bay at RAF Binbrook as they wanted to learn from the damage. The transport cost was considerable, but this was not the time to lose our very few remaining friends.

A few days later I had a late-night call from John Watkins. 'What do you want me to do with the engine now, Richard?' I explained that we were desperately short of funds had no obvious way forward, and suggested the engine remains be dumped in a local scrapyard.

'Now why would you want to do that, Richard? When the engine bay has worked nights rebuilding your engine and the Queen has paid for the parts.'

This was brilliant good fortune, and we could go forward again. There is a rumour that the engine internals are all branded with the personal thoughts of the engine bay night shift.

It wasn't until I reread Mike Barrett's book thirty-nine years later that I was reminded the critical red V-12 Jaguar marker car had been swapped for a brown Range Rover at the last minute before the run. I had been briefed on the swap, but in haste had forgotten. The red Jaguar, my all-important 220-mph braking point, was never there.

Mike Barrett took over the leadership of the island workshop team and, with a supreme team effort, Thrust 2 was rebuilt in twelve intense weeks, ready to go back to Bonneville.

Now, the immediate action was to test run the rebuilt car and transport the car's team and vehicles to Bonneville. We had concluded that Bonneville was the only place for the high speed – all the local resources and experience were on site and, after all, we had seen 500 mph on the Bonneville salt the year before.

When we arrived at Wendover, Utah, we met heavy rain. The salt immediately flooded and John and I went swimming. There was no way that Bonneville would dry again in 1982. We had lost our opportunity with the crash – or had we? Rumour had it that the sponsors had all signed up to the pluvious insurance…

Thrust 2's post-accident twelve-week rebuild at Ranalagh, 1982.

Washout! Bonneville floods again. Time to find another site. (1982)

On 28 September we were having a solemn lunchtime team meeting in the Stateline Casino when Peter Moore, a displaced Brit who had come to see Thrust 2 run, joined and asked Ken, 'What do you guys really need?'

Ken explained, 'We need an alkali or salt desert with a run of 11–13 miles of smooth, flat, accessible with a hard surface – and dry.'

Peter Moore explained that he loved the American deserts and had frequently flown over them in his private Beech T-34 Mentor military trainer over many years.

'There are two candidates for you,' he said. 'Alvord Desert in Oregon and the Black Rock Desert in Nevada.'

John and Charles Noble immediately set off for Alvord, and Pete and I for the long haul to Black Rock. We would report back to the team as soon as we could. There might just be a chance lurking somewhere and, with winter on the way, every minute counted.

Chapter 8
Black Rock Desert and It's Still 1982

Of the two possible desert lakebeds, we went for Black Rock. The desert is a 200-square-mile alkali playa brown desert with a naturally perfect flat surface, which is washed level by the annual winter rainfall. As the water evaporates with the summer heat the winds blow the remaining water around the desert surface, which generates the flat surface – a sort of annual plastering job. The actual surface consists of zillions of small platelets composed of many thousands of years of micro-silt particles washed down from the Sierra Nevada mountains over the millennia. When baked hard by the sun it performs like a mattress, providing a springy but load-bearing surface. The surface is probably more draggy than the hard salt of Bonneville, but it works much better for the solid wheels. Simply put, the surface provides the flexy compliance that you would normally expect from a car tyre.

Hard surface run lengths of up to 13 miles are possible. The Black Rock Desert is just over 120 miles north of Reno, Nevada, and the local town is Gerlach.

Key to all this is the fact that the annual flooding completely obliterates any tracks made from Thrust 2 high-speed runs. The surface renews every winter, and the Thrust 2 environmental impact is non-existent. So, we have a sustainable operation.

John Ackroyd explained the benefits: 'Did you know that Thrust 2 gets a smoother run here at 500 mph than when it is on its transporter!'

Learning from the Bonneville experience, John equipped Thrust 2 with new front wheels with a 6-inch-wide tread, which was to make a huge difference to handling.

The team arrived on 4 October 1982 and by the 7th the US Bureau of Land Management had issued a preliminary short-term operating licence, so any surface damage to the desert could be assessed.

The team and local friends quickly got Thrust 2 operational on the desert. Key to this was the use of Walt Ashton's Cessna 182, which was used for desert track-spotting duties. As usual, Mile Barrett was loading the brake chutes. Mike Hearn and John Griffiths were providing fire cover with the Jaguar Firechase.

With winter coming, the team were already on borrowed time and the productive pace had to be fast. Thrust 2 speeds were ramped up quickly to over 400 mph on the new and better surface. But all the preparations were brought to a halt on the 15 October. The extreme environmentalist group Sierra Club demanded that the BLM

Thrust 2 unloads at Cecil Courtney's Texaco garage, Gerlach, 1982.

On the Black Rock for the first time. (1982)

Walt's Cessna, 182 track spotter. (1982)

Jaguar Firechase team: Mike Hearn and John Griffiths, 1982.

Thrust 2 ready for the start Black Rock, 1982.

licence be withdrawn on environmental grounds and that the entire programme be brought to a halt. But, amazingly, the citizens of the two local towns, Gerlach and Empire, rose to the challenge and presented a counter petition with 600 signatures, which was quickly accepted by local congressman Jim Santini. The petition was presented on television and the restriction lifted. It was a terrific performance by the local people. The team was now free to push on to maximise performance, with the only restrictions being engineering, finance and the weather.

By 19 October the runs had only made a peak of 400 mph and there were suspect afterburner problems. Eddie Elsom quickly had the situation under control. The nearest air force base was Fallon Naval Base, near Reno. Eddie was still negotiating with the base commander when the Thrust 2 arrived on its transporter and passed his office window.

'So, OK, when are you coming?' asked the station commander. Eddie: 'Err, I thinks that's us now!'

The Fallon US Navy executives generously allowed the team to tie down the car at its fighter run-up site. Late that night Thrust was showing a 30-foot exhaust plume together with 'the dancing diamonds' – supersonic exhaust flames.

Of course, the winter rain was on its way and could reduce the desert to brown, sticky porridge at a stroke, making it impassable, even for a Range Rover. Even by repositioning the timekeeper's measured mile to allow more of a run-up distance, it

Night reheat testing, US Fallon Naval Base, Nevada, 1983.

Thrust 2 at 600 mph, Black Rock Desert, 1982.

was quite clear that the 1982 programme was drawing to an inevitable close. But on 4 November we saw a new average of 590.551 mph for the two passes and a peak of 615 mph. The relentless pressure was getting to the team, and at the team meeting that night John Ackroyd made the point that we had been under continuous strain since the Greenham crash and it hadn't relaxed for a single day since. 'I've had it,' he said.

The decision point came the next morning – 5 November – when it started to snow and it was clear that the 1982 programme was over. We had to be satisfied with a peak of 615 mph and an average of 590.551 mph for the mile. We had pushed car and weather to the absolute limit.

It was time to repack and take the long trail back to the UK. The year 1982 had been an amazing one of team achievement. The Greenham accident had set the programme back, but because we were forced to reposition at Black Rock we got better results than if we had spent our time on the Bonneville Salt Flats. Thrust 2 was now in the 600 mph range and in with a real chance.

The 1982 publicity for the sponsors was seriously valuable, including more television coverage and, of course, the sponsors had committed to another pluvious insurance, so if they agreed then there was just a chance we might be able to continue the fight and run again in 1983. We were inching closer to Faberge's gold standard.

The final run reached 615 mph, but this was not fast enough. (1982)

Rain again! The desert turns to mud. (1982)

Chapter 9
The Big Cliffhanger and John Acker's Three Fixes

It's January 1983, Thrust 2 is back on the island and the team are back after an incredibly demanding year. We had pushed everything and everyone to the limit and there had been no walkouts. We were privileged to have a truly exceptional team. Thrust 2 had made 615 mph; it's true that's a top speed and should not be compared with Blue Flame's 622 mph, which was a mile average, but the potential difference was closing. But make no mistake, making up that speed difference with a car that was already closing on its peak speed and in the high drag transonic speed range was going to be no easy challenge.

But while 1982 was a hectic struggle against time, 1983 promised something different. Unlike the Bonneville experience in 1981, the car was not caked with salt and corroded. The alkali Black Rock Desert just provided a fine dust, which, of course, got everywhere. Taking a predictive guess at the Black Rock Desert's climate, the earliest it could be expected to be dry again would be in August – actually, we were finally back on the desert by 12 September. It might look like an easy period for the team, but it wasn't. The 1982 car performance was marginal and we had to make up the considerable difference with many changes. And then there was the money to consider: would the sponsor companies still support us, or would we need to have the agony of refinancing again? And then there was the engine power to review. The plan was obvious and it was just as Leo Villa had said: more power, less drag and less weight.

John Ackroyd's plan was to lighten the car where possible, to reduce the drag from the underside of the car where the desert dust mixed with the supersonic airflow generating considerable underside drag. We also needed to see what Rolls-Royce could do with more adjustments to the Avon 302 engine.

Of course, we couldn't wait for the sponsors' decision, so we pushed ahead quickly. Mike Barrett was to spend two months under the car, stripping out the entire underside and making up additional fairings for the front wheels and for the trailing arm rear suspension.

John was keen to have the car repainted. After the Greenham accident there had been a partial repaint and John was aware there was now too much paint. Our sponsor Trimite generously agreed to strip the car and then repaint, and once again we saw Thrust 2 in its beautiful bare aluminium.

The repaint went wrong. Somehow the paint contractors lost confidence in the job and the result was a total mess. Our beautiful car now looked a complete wreck – there were colour changes, paint runs, oversprays curtains and sags. Thanks to Brian Balls' efforts the car was quickly stripped again and repainted by British Aerospace at Hurn Airport to a superb standard, and that's the beautiful paint the car sports to this day – thirty-nine years later.

The attention now had to turn to the Rolls-Royce 302 engine. From the early days, we had all known there was a challenge here. Earlier performance predictions had suggested that the afterburning engine thrust was likely to take a slight dip around 600 mph, just when the aero drag was increasing with the onset of transonic drag and when the car needed additional powerful acceleration to reach higher speeds. There was a real chance that without substantial change the car might never go faster than 620 mph. To beat the Blue Flame record we needed an average of 629 mph.

The engine was quickly sent to Rolls-Royce at East Kilbride for attention and reset so that the rotational speed could be increased by about 2 per cent above the maximum allowable. This would increase the amount of air going through the engine and produce another 1,600 lbs of engine thrust. This extra airflow meant that the fuel flow to the afterburner could also be increased, and its exit nozzle increased in

The Thrust 2 team, from left to right: Ron Benton, John Ackroyd, Geoff Smee (background), Gordon Flux, Mike Barrett and Eddie Elsom.

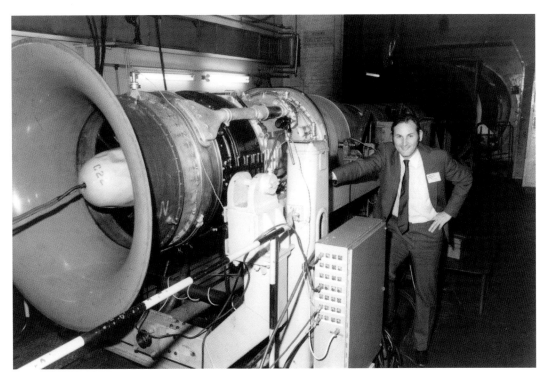

Avon 302 looking for max power, Rolls-Royce, East Kilbride, 1983.

area. This would all be extra power at the critical 600–620-mph speed range. All this extra power would require more fuel – were our tanks big enough? Perhaps we should have increased the fuel tankage, but we didn't. There were two more essential changes needed, but these would come later – when desperate, needs must.

In discussions with the Rolls-Royce team I asked them how long they had run the engine in max reheat: 'About an hour,' they said. I didn't ask where the fuel bill was going; I just hoped it wasn't coming our way.

We decided not to go back to Greenham Common (the site of the 1982 crash) for testing. The team felt there was no need to risk the car again in the UK after work was completed. High-performance UK runs on the short runways were now seen as too risky and really there was minimal relevance – the car was now only happy above 600 mph.

Back in Nevada, the Bureau of Land Management had to consider issuing a new permit to run for 1983 and, as a government organisation, they had to invite public interest. John and I went over to give evidence and after the public discussions the permit was formally issued. It helped enormously that John was a keen environmentalist and could give a balanced and reasoned argument. It also helped that the team had worked closely with the Bureau and had cleared the desert thoroughly after 1982 and was seen as a responsible organisation.

By now the team had decided to get out to Nevada at the earliest opportunity, but the problem was that of deciding when was this would be. It all depended on the desert drying and there was no formula for prediction. Even more difficult was assessing the desert condition from local reports. Now that the car was ready to go the solution was for John to reposition in Gerlach and take a much-prized early Hewlett Packard fax machine (the size of small cabin trunk) with him. We could communicate by sketches.

Weeks passed and John Ackroyd's faxes showed very slow drying progress while the team was on standby in the UK. It was said that there had been years when the desert, usually flooded from meltwater in the Sierra Nevada mountains, never dried, so there was a worry that Project Thrust was finished. I wasn't sure whether this was covered in the sponsors' pluvious insurance policy.

'One Take' Watkins and Brian Ball arrive at Gerlach, Nevada, 1983.

Eddie Elsom, the great fixer! (1983)

Ken Norris, the project chairman, 1983.

However, by early September the team was on its way, and five days after arrival Thrust 2 made its first powered run. By Run 3 – on the 20th – Thrust 2 was at 590-mph peak speed. The car felt very different with much greater acceleration.

By Run 7 – 23 September – we were in trouble. It looked as though the engine had surged: a nasty experience where the airflow in the engine explosively reverses and fire comes out the intake. The speed was 607 mph, and it was clear that Thrust 2's performance had peaked. Not only was this bad news and possibly the end of the project, but all this happened in front of our VIP visitor Gary Gabelich, then holder of the world record at 622.407 mph. Gabelich was very gracious and friendly, but we got the impression he didn't believe his record was in any sort of danger. I think he saw us as beginners still struggling with an unlikely car.

He looked over Thrust 2 and couldn't really understand what he was looking at. The Blue Flame was a fine, thin, aerodynamic missile on wheels; Thrust 2 must have looked like a streamlined brick.

'What do you think of Thrust 2?' he was asked by the TV crew. Gabelich struggled with a non-committal reply. 'It's nice' was all he could manage.

The crew filmed an interview with him and he explained that record-breaking was all about struggle and never giving up. Gabelich had been fortunate. He got his record on his team's first Bonneville event. Thrust 2 was on its third event. There was nothing Gabelich could tell the Thrust team about perseverance.

Thrust 2 tracks, laser straight at Black Rock, 1983.

But the Thrust team was in deep trouble already. There was possible engine damage and the car's performance had plateaued. The project was probably over. We needed immediate help.

John Watkins, the project's engine specialist, had been stuck at his base at RAF Binbrook smartening the place up for a royal visit. Given the crisis, the Royal Air Force responded by quickly releasing him to travel.

We sent the Rolls-Royce main board in London a summary of the situation and performance readings. Without their help, the project had made its last run. The board was not at all pleased at being approached in this way, but they appreciated the crisis and Lancastrian George Webb was immediately sent on his way to us from Rolls-Royce Atlanta.

George and John Watkins hit it off immediately, and the message to the team was that there was no evidence of molten aluminium in the jet exhaust and the engine had not surged; in fact, it was intact. The project could fight another day.

They were worried about the fuel-to-air ratio, but during their inspection they were surprised to find an engine installation fault. The multistage reheat system was unable to open up to full reheat because of a quadrant control design error, so the engine had never been at full power in the car.

This was easily fixed and Thrust 2 was taken to a military jet fighter tie down at nearby Reno airport. With help from an airport fire team the engine was run up and George blasted the intake with a steady jet of water from the airport fire truck. A stream of muddy water poured out from the intake. We ran more afterburner trials, and it was clear that for once in the project's lifetime the afterburner flame actually filled the jet exhaust. For the first time we had a full house power delivery from the Avon 302.

Full reheat at long, long last. Reno, 1983.

Of course, crises never seem to come as single events. We had been operational on the desert for sixteen days and the project was running out of money. Richard Chisnell from Initial was with us and was known as 'The Sponsor'. He had generously given up a month of his time representing the other sponsors. Running out of money is a serious business at any time, but even more serious when on the desert. Any inability to pay our suppliers would wreck our local goodwill and seriously endanger the project. And there was still very real doubt about our ability to achieve the record. Richard Chisnell created a very accurate and honest report, which went back to the sponsors with an ask for a further £20,000 to keep going. Seven sponsors agreed and were immediately labelled 'the Magnificent Seven', and there was a further tranche of £20,000. This was hugely valuable support for the team at a time when we were beset with major problems on almost every front.

It was now 29 September and it looked as though we would be unable to run because of crosswinds. As if by a miracle the wind dropped and starting from the draggy northern end of the track. Thrust 2 was away on Run 8.

It felt like a new car: there was suddenly hard and sharp acceleration. The car had a new purpose in life, and we got a mile speed of 622. We tried for Run 9, but we had to abort. The engine had not stabilised, and the afterburner would not select. We were not out of the woods yet, but perhaps we were heading in the right direction.

John Watkins checked over the reheat system and found air in the feed pipes. It was thought that the problem was fuel starvation. Bleed points for the engine and reheat pumps were now made. Perhaps we should have enlarged the tanks when the car was in the workshop after all. It was far too late to make major changes now – time, money and weather were running out.

At the team meeting that night John Ackroyd hit on the cause. Thrust 2 has two 62-gallon fuel tanks: the starboard one for the engine and the port tank for the fueldraulic afterburner system. There is a bridge pipe between the two tanks. Post-run checks would show that the port tank would empty faster than the starboard. Ackroyd theorised that because the car was now developing much more power, the fuel tanks were emptying faster. This meant that, with the savage 5 g-force deceleration car and driver were experiencing, the remaining fuel in the tanks was rushing forward, uncovering the tank fuel pump's intakes, and the pumps were sucking in air. He thought that the air was being drawn in via the tank breather – curiously, one of the first parts of the car to be made. The solution was to keep the starboard pump on for longer to balance out the fuel flows and to bleed the systems when the car came to a halt on the turnaround. A timer for the pump was quicky precured and the bleed points established. It would be easy to surmise that, with the uprated engines, the tanks were only just marginally large enough. With no more capacity available the timed pump was the last possible fix.

John had three more fixes in his mind, and we now had to try them all, as we were close to the end of the season. It could rain and flood the desert anytime now.

The first was to fit the narrower tread width front wheels, which had caused us so much trouble at Bonneville. The idea was that the narrower Bonneville wheels would cause less aero drag and enable higher speeds. The idea was a clunk: the narrow front wheels dug into the desert surface and all the hopeless Bonneville handling problems returned at 480 mph. They were returned to their boxes.

The next ideas were to raise the incidence of the car by 0.17 of a degree nose up to release some of the download on the front wheels and reduce the rolling resistance. This was a controversial move because even a slight adjustment it could trigger a rapid loss of download at the front, which might switch the car into a sudden transonic backflip. We had no time or resource to model this and we would have to accept the risk. The weight on the front wheels at speed was 6,360 lbs before the change and 3,680 lbs after. We were very nearly caught out because the later performance curves would show that the front of the car was unloading very smartly with speed – the car was within 7 mph of take off at 650 mph. The situation would become really dangerous when the engine, with its afterburner downthrust moment, was cancelled at maximum speed. In the cockpit there was absolutely no indication that the car was about to fly.

John's third idea was to understand that the car was Mach number limited. If right, this meant that the car could only reach a given Mach number (the Mach number defines the airspeed as a percentage of the local speed of sound). As the driver I preferred driving in the early morning, as the temperature was lower, the visibility better and my mind was clearer. But the temperature was lower and that depressed the speed of sound and affected our maximum speed.

So, our problem lay with the Mach number– in other words, because of transonic wave drag the car would go no faster than Mach 0.84. The speed of sound is proportional to local temperature – the hotter the day, the higher the airspeed for a given Mach No. So, if we could run in the hottest part of the day, the car's maximum speed would be much higher. As an example, on an earlier run the car had peaked at 622 mph and Mach 0.834 at a local temperature of 43° F. If we were to run at a higher temperature, say 73° F at Mach 0.834, we should see 643 mph.

So now we move forward to 4 October 1983. The Thrust 2 car was now at its best condition ever, the car was run with a positive incidence and the fuel system was sorted. All we had to do was go out and get the world land speed sound). It had taken nine years to reach the pinnacle.

The first runs started on the draggy north desert with a flat-out run of 5½ miles, reaching 632 mph in 55 seconds with an average of 624.241 mph through the mile. To the team, it didn't seem fast enough.

We turned the car around well within the hour, and this time we were on the harder southern end surface with a 6⅛-mile run into the measured mile and the temperate suddenly shot up to 75° F, raising the speed of sound in our favour. The car was on full song; the engine and afterburner roared as never before and, curiously, my helmet began to rattle on the head rest, in the process ratcheting up my Panotex fireproof head sock so that the eye holes gradually moved upwards over my cheeks and I had to incline my head to be able to see through the eye slots. The car felt brilliant as we roared through the measured mile with the usual shockwaves over the wheel arches and the intake, followed by the usual 5.5-g somatogravic decels. It was a good run, but it didn't feel any better than Run 9. But it was! The average through the mile was 642.971 mph, with an incredible peak speed of 650.88 mph.

All those years ago, in 1977, we had set the Thrust 2 target at 650 mph and we had fractionally exceeded it – what an incredible team effort. Don Macgregor's (the USAC timing official) radio comment will be with the team for the rest of our lives: 'Time for the Mile 5.599 seconds Speed 642.971 mph – it's a new record, congratulations.' And two days later there was an unexpected evening fax for us on the enormous yellow Hewlett Packard fax machine:

To Mr Richard Noble
I was very pleased to hear of your success in recapturing the World Land Speed Record
I send you and all your team my hearty congratulations.

Elizabeth R
6th October 1983

Our American friends were impressed and, for the team, our lives would never be the same again. Against all the odds and with nine years of seemingly endless struggle, Britain once again held the world's land speed record at 633.468 mph for the mile.

Chapter 10
Author's Review, 2022

I would like to thank the publisher for giving us all an opportunity to have another look at the Thrust 2 project. They gave us a very prescriptive instruction and it was for a short and tight narrative. Earlier books have provided the reader with more meat, such as the exceptional David Tremayne's *The Fastest Man on Earth*, a brilliant, enjoyable and incredibly accurate and perceptive record.

A lifetime's celebration.

Car sticker.

When we finally completed the Thrust 2 programme, timekeeper Dave Petrali, a legendary man of few words, who with his famous father had timed almost all the land speed records since the 1930s, gave it to me straight: 'When this team started with us on Bonneveille back in 1981, we saw you all as the greenest and most inexperienced team we had ever timed. When we recorded the record this week, we unanimously decided you were the most capable and professional team we had ever experienced.'

This book gives us the opportunity to review what was achieved nearly forty years ago. Many of the team have passed on, including John Ackroyd, Ken Norris, Brian Ball, Mike Barrett, and others. The idea of this book is to review what happened in the light of our later experience with projects and, make no mistake, without the extraordinary success of Thrust 2 there might have been no more projects to follow.

The key to Thrust 2's success was the fact that at the start we all admitted we had no relevant experience in relation to designing, building and operating a transonic record breaker. There was little to learn from the Bluebird CN-7 record of 1964 – thirteen years before and 230 mph slower – and this meant that absolutely every aspect had to be learned. Nothing was to be assumed and, as John so often said, 'We started with a clean sheet of paper.' That meant every aspect of the project had to be argued from first principles, and John shut himself away in the derelict Ranalagh kitchen and worked it all out piecemeal. With his apprentice background of high-performance aerodynamics and a subsequent happy-go-lucky approach he had probably come to the conclusion that he needed to prove himself with an outstanding engineering opportunity for personal achievement and with a small, highly focussed team. We were all glad to give him the opportunity.

John thought through, argued out, designed and implemented almost every aspect of the Thrust 2 design by himself. We all quickly found that whenever we came up with what we thought was an original idea John had got there first, had all the arguments in place and had already implemented the decision. Thrust 2 was very much John's car, and it was unfortunate that the visionless people who handed out medals, despite prompting, failed to acknowledge his brilliant work.

The project, of course, depended on many others, all providing essential support to the main project team, and over 200 companies were involved.

A very important element that held us all together was the team's humour, led by 'One Take' Watkins, Brian Ball, Mike Barrett and Andrew Noble. There was a constant flow of superb humour, which kept us all hugely enjoying the experience, despite all the project's immense struggles and endless difficulties.

Undoubtedly, the best example of this was Ron Benton's 1983 record attempt seated on a portable potty, towed through the measured mile and officially timed by our very professional and experienced USAC timekeepers at 54 mph. Covered in stray lavatory paper, Ron Benton announced, in a 1930s theatrical voice, that his next attempt would be the sound barrier. Our American friends weren't quite sure about the importance of all this, but the Thrust team were doubled up in laughter.

We got the all-important team structure right, though not intentionally. John did the engineering, I made the money, and together we kept the early programme moving. But when I moved on to start developing the driving, we both needed help. I tried to manage the project and drive the car at Bonneville in 1981, but the two roles were not compatible and I very nearly made a mess of the entire project. It was John's idea to bring in Ken Norris to manage the team on the desert trials and it turned out to be a brilliant move, so let's start right there.

Ken Norris, a very quiet, sensible and mature engineer, had been through the record mill before several times, designing Donald Campbell's successful K7 boat and CN-7 land speed record car. Strangely, Ken would never talk about the Campbell experience, which suggests it wasn't necessarily a happy one. But there was one revealing moment when on the desert with Thrust 2 in the 600s. I suggested that perhaps as an encore we should restore the CN-7 and see whether we could achieve the CN-7 500-mph design speed. Ken was deeply thrilled with the idea, but regrettably it never happened.

John preferred a hierarchical design and build team with him leading the key engineering decisions. He was supported by the brilliant ex-RAF team of Tony Meston and Geoff Smee, who threw in their lot in with him and individually handled the early electrics (later taken over by Gordon Biles), the crucial Avon 210 engine installation and early testing. Key support came from the master craftsmen Ron Benton, Mike Barrett and Brian Ball. It's important to understand that these brilliant craftsmen recruited us, not the other way around. John ran a tight ship during the design and build, but something different was required on the desert in 1982 and 1983. We had no land speed record team operational experience, and Ken supplied it in his quiet Ken way of doing things. On the desert he ran an all-inclusive flat operation where everyone was listened to and the best decisions were implemented. This worked so well that there were no team politics and there was huge respect for the leadership of this quiet and outstanding engineer.

Ken also had another role, which was key to the success of the entire project. I had done the selling job to bring the sponsors into the programme, but somehow they had to be kept aboard through the inevitable failures and successes. The sponsors were committing large sums from their annual promotional budgets, so there was real risk and they had never expected a long, drawn-out programme. Ken very kindly agreed to chair the monthly sponsors' UK meetings, where he provided independent engineering explanation and judgement to the sponsors who by now had moved on from my intense sales pitches. With the exception of the Faberge team, they stayed with the project right through to the successful end.

We also need to record the work of Glyn Bowsher, who together with Lucas Girling designed and made the wheel brakes, which although designed for use from 200 mph had to withstand the rotational speed of 8,000 rpm (over 650 mph). We had minimal problems with the brakes and the special lubricated wheel bearings. Glyn's reports were the most thorough engineering reports we were privileged to read. His photos were the best and I am proud to have then on our walls at home. Glyn was to join us in the 1997 ThrustSSC project, where we broke the sound barrier.

We need to talk about Initial Services too, our main sponsor, who provided the financial backbone of the entire project. At that time Initial Services was a highly successful group of laundries, which all depended on manual labour for loading and unloading giant washing machines. Tony Waring saw the project on a BBC programme and decided that an association with this hugely ambitious programme might provide a powerful workforce stimulant. Director Henry Lewis backed the deal and Richard Chisnell was our prime contact. In 1980, when we had a sponsor walkout due to finances, Henry solemnly doubled the sponsorship fee and saved both the project and the day. Later, when we finally succeeded, the Initial board were surprised to find far better than expected annual accounts, but they couldn't account for it. It seemed that the association with Thrust had so stimulated the workforce that the benefits actually showed in the annual accounts. This was totally unexpected, but the board had not set up a system to monitor the project's influence, so they could never explain it. As such, it remains merely a rumour.

Out on the desert in 1983 the project was running out of funding, and it was Richard Chisnell who represented the sponsors and who persuaded them that an immediate £20,000 was needed. Seven financial sponsors willingly took us all through to the last phase and they will always to be known as 'the Magnificent Seven'.

It makes interesting reading to review what might have happened differently if a different set of dice had been thrown. It demonstrates just how critical the balance of events has to be to result in success.

Firstly, John's decision to use twin tailfins was hugely beneficial above 300 mph. In 1981, once on the Bonneville Salt Flats, Thrust 2 started as a nasty and unpredictable beast. 60 per cent of the weight was on the front skinny wheels, which broke through the salt to the hard subsurface below. From my point of view, I faced driving a car when the steering had minimal effect and the car threatened to depart sideways without warning. A car going sideways at those speeds was likely to fly, so I didn't want to add reheat power to an already unstable and unpredictable vehicle. The 400-mph runs appeared much better, but we experienced a long drag to actually get to 400 mph without the afterburner. I used reheat in anger when the teamwork failings became embarrassingly obvious on the all-important trial turnaround and the car suddenly ran straight. What we had discovered was that John's tailfins gave us good stability above 300 mph and, extraordinarily, the afterburner gave us much better low-speed stability. It was all completely unexpected and a real shame that Bonneville chose to flood the next day and cut short the hard-earned promising development. But it gave us an insight to what might be possible for 1982.

Perhaps we were gifted a key opportunity when it rained at Bonneville in 1982 and we had to find another venue. Certainly, the wheel drag was greater on Black Rock Desert, but at least the new solid wheels worked well and gave us all great confidence.

Real danger can lurk in these long, drawn-out programmes. After a period of intense stress, the inner compulsion is to enjoy a period of relaxation. This happened in 1983 when it became clear that the Black Rock would take time to dry, and John Akroyd was enjoying his time in the desert reporting on the process. Hindsight, of course, is an exact science and we had two problems of which we were unaware and could have failed the project. And we lost the time to fix one of them. For the record runs we must have known that the final runs would need longer acceleration runs and that the newly reset Avon 302 engine would require much more fuel for its increased power. We failed to increase the size of the fuel tanks in the time available and the record was only achieved by Mike Hearne's brilliant idea to fit a timer for the engine fuel pump, thus making more fuel available for the reheat from the port tank – an absolutely brilliant and innovative solution, which cost us minimal time on the desert, but made the record possible.

The 1980 British Aerospace transonic wind tunnel tests were a huge bonus to the project and a conviction for us all that John's unusual design could achieve 650 mph when the media were saying that we needed a Blue Flame-like missile shape. We all failed to understand that the car was Mach number limited, and that we couldn't expect it to go faster than Mach 0.84 under any circumstances. As the driver I preferred early morning starts when the air was cool for the engine and the visibility at its best. This was plain wrong; we might have progressed a lot faster if we had decided to run in the hottest part of the day when the same Mach number meant considerably more groundspeed.

The Rolls-Royce Avon 302 and its afterburner was a crucial part of the story. The car was originally powered with the Avon 210 engine. I suggested we upgrade to the Avon 302, which meant major changes to engine afterburner, starter and fuel system. Somehow the essential control linkage to the 302 afterburner was not correctly understood and this meant that the largest jet pipe reheat gutter was never selected for 1982 and some of 1983. So, all the 1982 runs could have been a lot faster. Of course, we had noted that the reheat flame never filled the jet pipe, but we thought this was normal. While we could have gone a lot faster in 1982 if we had got this right, there was a very serious downside to this. During the 1982 Greenham accident we were using what we thought was max reheat and mistakenly peaked at over 300 mph on the 1.9-mile runway. If we'd had the benefit of the correctly installed reheat, we might have been nearer to 400 mph and Mike Barrett and I might not have survived the experience.

As it was it took George Webb, sent to Black Rock by the Rolls-Royce board, just a few hours to spot the problem. If the board had not bothered to send George, we would have failed.

But the biggest mistake of all was mine. I failed to record on that fateful June day on Greenham Common that the red Jaguar trackside marker had been replaced by a brown Range Rover and spent too long at over 300 mph looking for the non-existent Jaguar. That set the entire 1982 programme back twelve weeks for the rebuild and induced huge stress in the team. All this shows just how critical success really is.

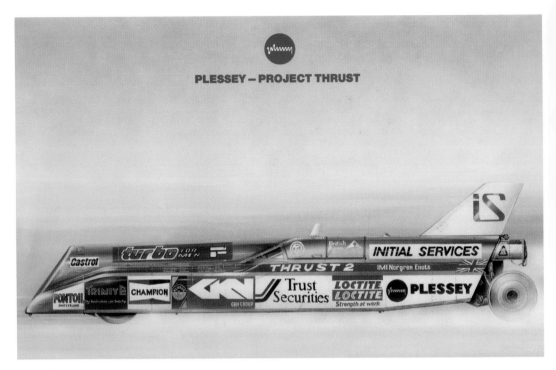

Thrust 2, 1983.

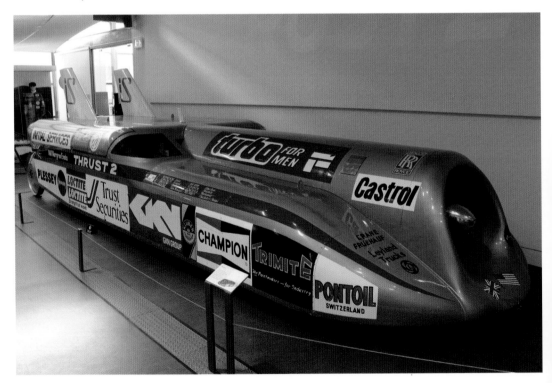

Thrust 2 at Coventry Transport Museum. (Karl Schneidau)

The Team and The Records

1983 record team

John Ackroyd	Designer
Ken Norris	Team Manager
Eddie Elsom	Operations Director
Gordon Flux	Chief Engineer
Mike Barrett	Parachutes
Gordon Biles	Electrics
John Watkins	Engine team leader
Brian Ball	Build team bodywork development
Glynne Bowsher	Brakes
Mick Chambers	Wheel bearings
Andrew Noble	Transporter Driver
Ron Benton	Build Team bodywork development
David Brinn	Financial Director
Peter Hand	Electronics
John Griffiths	Fire Chase Jaguar team
Mike Hearn	Fire Chase Jaguar Team
David Tremayne	Press and PR manager
Ian Robinson	Track prep team
John Norris	Track Prep team
Charles Noble	Photographer
Sally Noble	Supporters Club Secretary
Birgit Ackroyd	Team Secretary
Ton Palm	Start team
Richard Chisnell	Sponsors representative
Simon Walmesly	Electronics
George Webb	Rolls-Royce (engine team)
Richard Noble	Director and Driver

United States Auto Club Timekeepers

Dave Petrali	Chief Steward
Buck Wetton	Chief Timer
Jess Tobey	Chief Observer
Mac MacGregor	Tech Representative

Reproduced with thanks from Fastest Man On Earth

Thrust 2 British and World Records

24 and 25 September 1980
Site: RAF Greenham Common Newbury, Berks UK

1 Mile Standing Start	166.47 mph
1 Kilometre Standing Start	149.57 mph
¼ mile Flying Start	259.74mph
500 metres Flying Start	255.06 mph
1 kilometre Flying Start	251.19 mph
1 mile Flying Start	248.87 mph

World Unlimited, 04.10.83, Black Rock Desert	Mile	633.468 mph
American Unlimited, 04.10.83, Black Rock Desert	Mile	633.468 mph
International Group C Jet, 04.10.83, Black Rock Desert	Mile	633.468 mph
National Cat C Group Jet, 04.10.83, Black Rock Desert	Mile	633.468 mph

Kilometre Speed – 634.051 mph. While faster than existing records, this was not official as it did not exceed the previous record by the mandatory one per cent.

Reproduced with thanks from The Fastest Man on Earth.